Praise for Barry Forshaw

'Entertaining and informative companion… written by the person who probably knows more than anyone alive about the subject' — **Marcel Berlins,** *The Times*

'Fascinating and well researched… refreshing and accessible' — **Russel McLean,** *The Herald*

'Highly accessible guide to this popular genre' — **Nicholas Bieber,** *Daily Express*

'He is the perfect guide, effortlessly taking us across time and space' — **Stav Sherez,** *Catholic Herald*

'As always, Forshaw's books are fascinating to read and provide a handy insight into new authors to try' — *Crime Pieces*

'Far more than a checklist, this is the essential guide through the snowdrifts of Nordic noir' — **Val McDermid, author of** *The Wire in the Blood,* **on** *Death in a Cold Climate*

'Readers wanting to get into Scandinavian crime fiction should start with Forshaw's pocket guide to the genre' — **Christopher Fowler,** *Financial Times*

'Provides an eminently readable, interesting and informative overview of this hugely popular and varied branch of crime fiction' — **Mystery People**

T0051592

Praise for *Crime Fiction: A Reader's Guide*

'Essential reading for anyone seeking clues' – *Guardian*

'This guided meander through the field of crime
fiction offers many pleasures of surprise and discovery'
– **Emma Kareno,** *Times Literary Supplement*

'Essentially a crime writing equivalent to the much-missed
Halliwell's Film Guide and all the better for it'
– **Sarah Hughes,** *i news*

'The perfect book and present for any crime fiction lovers
out there' – **Liz Robinson,** *LoveReading*

'He leaves no stone unturned… Essential' – *Crime Monthly*

'At a time when critical negativity often seems depressingly
fashionable, his constructive approach comes as a breath of
fresh air' – **Martin Edwards, author of** *Gallows Court*

'This well considered volume is essential to navigate
literature's darkest avenue' – **Ali Karim,** *Shots Mag*

'A useful study that deserves a place in the library
of all serious readers of crime fiction'
– **Woody Haut,** *Crime Time*

'It's a measure of Forshaw's writing style, a dose of wit, a
sharp observation, a pointed turn of phrase, that make it
possible to sit down and read this guide cover to cover with
real pleasure' – **Paul Burke,** *NB Magazine*

Also by Barry Forshaw

British Crime Writing: An Encyclopedia
British Crime Film
Nordic Noir
British Gothic Cinema
BFI War of the Worlds
Euro Noir
Sex and Film
Brit Noir
Italian Cinema
American Noir
Historical Noir
Crime Fiction: A Reader's Guide

SIMENON

THE MAN, THE BOOKS, THE FILMS

Barry Forshaw

OLDCASTLE BOOKS

First published in 2022 by Oldcastle Books,
Harpenden, UK
oldcastlebooks.co.uk
Copyeditor: Judith Forshaw

A CIP catalogue record for this book is available from the British Library.

ISBN
978-0-85730-416-2 (print)
978-0-85730-514-5 (ebook)

2 4 6 8 10 9 7 5 3 1

Typeset in 12.6 on 14.4pt Perpetua
by Avocet Typeset, Bideford, Devon, EX39 2BP
Printed and bound by CPI Group (UK) Ltd, Croydon, CR0 4YY

For more information about Crime Fiction go to @crimetimeuk

CONTENTS

FOREWORD

Georges Simenon created a furore worthy of the most bed-hopping of politicians with his declaration that he had had sex with over 10,000 women. He made the claim in January 1977 in a conversation with Fellini in the magazine *L'Express* to launch Fellini's film *Casanova* in France, but the jaw-dropping statement was met with scepticism. How had he written so many novels if his entire time seems to have been spent in carnal abandon? Simenon admirers were alienated by what seemed like boastfulness – but, fortunately, it's not necessary to approve of all a writer's statements to admire his work. Leaving such things aside, by the time of his death in 1989, Simenon was the most successful writer of crime fiction in a language other than English in the entire field, and his most iconic creation, the pipe-smoking police inspector Jules Maigret, had become an institution. At the same time, his non-Maigret standalone novels are among the most commanding in the genre (notably *The Snow Was Dirty*, an unsparing analysis of the mind of a youthful criminal). Simenon created a writing legacy quite as substantial as many more 'serious' French literary figures; André Gide's assessment of him as 'the greatest French novelist of our times' may have been hyperbolic, but as a trenchant picture of French society, Simenon's books collectively forge a fascinating analysis.

But at this point, let's establish what this book isn't. It's not designed as a straightforward biography – I felt that a sort of 'collage' approach might fruitfully present a picture from various angles (the author's life and character, his remarkable literary achievements, and the many adaptations of his work in other media). To that end, apart from my own essays, I have interviewed a variety of people who either worked with him or worked on his books: publishers, editors, translators, and other specialist writers, some of whom I commissioned to write pieces on Simenon in the past for various books and magazines (notably *Crime Time*, which I have edited in both print and online formats). My hope is that all of this will create a prism through which to appreciate one of the most distinctive achievements in the whole of crime fiction.

Musical Chairs and Titles

At the heart of this study is a bibliography created by the late David Carter, which remains a very well-researched piece of work. Inevitably, of course, some of David's information reflected the time when it was written (2003), so I have customised a great many things – not least adding newly translated titles for books that have appeared previously under different monikers. A good example might be the first Maigret, originally published in 1931 as *Pietr-le-Letton* but subsequently appearing as both *Maigret and the Enigmatic Lett* and *The Case of Peter the Lett*, and which is now available under the more suitable title of *Pietr the Latvian* (in a translation by David Bellos). My yardstick in terms of titles has been the impressive Penguin initiative of new translations, which are unlikely to be bettered. I have kept some of David's plot synopses along with some of his value judgements, although, here again, I have added and subtracted extensively. Finally, though, as a starting point for this book, David's work has been extremely useful.

SIMENON: THE MAN

A One-Man Trojan Horse

Crime in translation may have achieved massive breakthroughs in the twenty-first century, but long before this trend, Simenon was a one-man Trojan horse in the field. Georges Joseph Christian Simenon was born in Liège on 13 February 1903; his father worked for an insurance company as a clerk, and his health was not good. Simenon found – like Charles Dickens in England before him – that he was obliged to work off his father's debts. The young man had to give up the studies he was enjoying, and he toiled in a variety of dispiriting jobs (including, briefly, working in a bakery). A spell in a bookshop was more congenial, as Simenon was already attracted to books, and his first experience of writing was as a local journalist for the *Gazette de Liège*. It was here that Simenon perfected the economical use of language that was to be a mainstay of his writing style; he never forgot the lessons he acquired in concision. Even before he was out of his teenage years, Simenon had published an apprentice novel and had become a leading figure in an enthusiastic organisation styling itself 'The Cask' (*La Caque*). This motley group of vaguely artistic types included aspiring artists and writers along with assorted hangers-on. A certain nihilistic approach to life was the philosophy of the group, and the transgressive pleasures of alcohol, drugs and sex were actively encouraged, with much discussion of these issues – and, of course, the arts were hotly debated. All of this offered a new excitement for the young writer after his sober teenage years. Simenon had always been attracted to women (and he continued to be enthusiastically so throughout his life) and in the early 1920s he married Régine Renchon, an aspiring young artist from his home town. The marriage, however, was troubled, although it lasted nearly 30 years.

From the City of Lights to the USA

Despite the bohemian delights of the Cask group, it was of course inevitable that Simenon would travel to Paris, which he did in 1922, making a career as a journeyman writer. In these early years, he published many novels and stories under a great variety of *noms de plume*.

Simenon took to the artistic life of Paris like the proverbial duck to water, submerging himself in all the many artistic delights at a time when the city was at a cultural peak, attracting émigré writers and artists from all over the world. He showed a particular predilection for the popular arts, starting a relationship with the celebrated American dancer Josephine Baker after seeing her many times in her well-known showcase *La Revue Nègre*. Baker was particularly famous for dancing topless, and this chimed with the note of sensuality that was to run through the writer's life. As well as sampling the fleshpots, along with more cerebral pursuits, Simenon became an inveterate traveller, and in the late 1920s he made many journeys on the canals of France and Europe.

There was an element of real-life adventure in Simenon's life at this time, when he became an object of attention for the police while in Odessa (where he had made a study of the poor). His notes from this time produced one of his most striking novels, *The People Opposite/Les Gens d'en Face* (1933), which was bitterly critical of the Soviet regime, which the author saw as corrupt. As the 1930s progressed, Simenon temporarily abandoned the police procedural novels featuring doughty Inspector Maigret (his principal legacy to the literary world), but he did not neglect his world travels, considering that the more experience of other countries he accrued, the better a writer he would be.

Like many people in France, Simenon's life was to change as the war years approached. In the late 1930s, he became Commissioner for Belgian Refugees at La Rochelle, and when France fell to the Germans, the writer travelled to Fontenay in the Vendée. His wartime experiences have always been a subject of controversy. Under the occupation, he added a new string to his bow when a group of films was produced under the Nazis based on his writing. It was, perhaps, inevitable that he would later be branded a collaborator, and this stain was to stay with him for the rest of his career. In the 1940s, while in Fontenay, Simenon became convinced that he was going to die when a doctor made an incorrect diagnosis based on an X-ray. Pierre Assouline's biography argues that this mistake was cleared up very quickly, but this erroneous sentence of death affected Simenon deeply and led to the writing of the autobiographical *Pedigree* about the writer's youth in Liège. The novel – Simenon's longest by far – was written between 1941 and 1943 but not published until 1948.

After the war, Simenon decided to relocate to Canada,

with a subsequent move to Arizona. The USA had become his home when he began a relationship with Denyse Ouimet, and his affair with this vivacious French Canadian was to be highly significant for him, inspiring the novel *Three Bedrooms in Manhattan/Trois Chambres à Manhattan* (1946). The couple married, and Simenon moved yet again, this time to Connecticut. This was a particularly productive period for him as a writer, and he created several works set in the USA, notably the powerful *Red Lights* in 1955, which, in its scabrous picture of the destructive relationship between a husband and wife, echoed the tough pulp fiction of James M. Cain. He also tackled organised crime in *The Brothers Rico/Les Frères Rico* in 1952 (subsequently filmed). However, always attracted by the prospect of a new relationship, Simenon began to neglect his wife and started an affair with a servant, Teresa Sburelin, with whom he set up house. (His wife Denyse spent some time in psychiatric clinics but outlived her husband by six years. She was a published author, and even practised as a psychiatrist for a time.)

In the 1950s, Simenon and his family returned to Europe, finally settling in a villa in Lausanne. Here, behind closed doors, he would enter an almost trancelike state, would write compulsively, usually completing an entire book in a week or two.

Simenon and Maigret

It quickly became clear that Simenon was the most successful writer of crime fiction (in a language other than English) in the entire genre, and his character Maigret had become as much of an institution as the author. The Simenon novels that can be described as standalones (i.e. books with no recurring detective figure) are among the most powerful in the genre, but there is absolutely no debate as to which of his creations is most fondly remembered: the pipe-smoking French Inspector of Police, Jules Maigret. The detective first appeared in the novel *Pietr the Latvian/Pietr-le-Letton* in 1931, and the author stated that he utilised characteristics that he had observed in his own great-grandfather. Almost immediately, all the elements that made the character so beloved were polished by the author: Commissaire in the Paris police headquarters at the Quai des Orfèvres, Maigret is a much more human figure than such great analytical detectives as Conan Doyle's Sherlock Holmes, and his approach to solving crimes is usually more dogged and painstaking than the inspired theatrics of other literary detectives. What Simenon introduced that was new in the field of detective fiction was to make his protagonist a quietly spoken observer of human nature, in which the techniques of psychology are focused on the various individuals he encounters – both the guilty and the innocent. Simenon gave his protagonist an almost therapeutic function, in which his job was to make people's lives better – although that usually involved the tracking down and (sometimes) the punishment of a criminal. Along with this concept of doing some good in society, Simenon decided that Maigret had initially wished to become a doctor but could not afford the necessary fees to achieve this goal. He also had Maigret working early in his career in the vice squad, but with little of the moral disapproval that was the establishment view of prostitution at the time (Madame de Gaulle famously sought – in vain – to have all the brothels in Paris closed down). Maigret, with his eternal sympathy for the victim, saw these women in that light and remained sympathetic, even in the face of dislike and distrust from the girls themselves. In *The Cellars of the Majestic/Les Caves du Majestic*, the detective has to deal with a prostitute who meets his attempts at understanding with scorn and insults. Whereas modern coppers such as Ian Rankin's Inspector Rebus are rebellious mavericks, eternally at odds with their superiors and battling such indulgences as alcoholism, Maigret is a classic example of the French bourgeoisie, ensconced in a contented relationship with his wife and less ostentatiously rebellious with authority – although he maintains a maverick sensibility. There is no alcoholism, but rather an appreciation of fine wines – and, of course, a cancer-defying relationship with a pipe (the sizeable pipe collection on his desk rivals Holmes's violin as a well-known detective accoutrement).

André Gide's famous encomium mentioned earlier ('the greatest French novelist of our times') may overstate the case, but the Maigret books provide us with a detailed picture of French society. There's social criticism here too – Maigret is always searching for the reasons behind crime, and sympathy is as much one of his qualities as his determination to see justice done.

Guilt and Innocence

Simenon inspired many writers of psychological crime, such as Patricia Highsmith; she once told me at a publisher's launch party in London that Simenon's name brightened her mood, whereas my mention of Hitchcock's film of her first book,

Strangers on a Train, definitely did not. Simenon's early thrillers featured psychological portrayals of loneliness, guilt and innocence that were at once acute and unsettling. *The Strangers in the House/Les Inconnus dans la Maison* (1940) depicts a recluse whose isolation is shattered by the discovery one night of a dead man in his house. The subsequent investigation draws this former lawyer back into humanity, to take on the case of the murderer himself. *The Man Who Watched the Trains Go By/L'Homme qui Regardait Passer les Trains* (1938) shows a normal family man, who, when the firm where he works collapses, becomes paranoid and capable of murder. He rushes towards his own extinction, determined for the world to appreciate his criminal genius.

Notions of guilt and innocence are central to the writer's world view, but rarely in a simple binary sense. Simenon sees the vagaries of human behaviour as complex: he is always ready to condemn egregious examples of malign behaviour, but he is equally ready to demonstrate flexibility when culpable actions can be viewed through a variety of prisms.

Simenon and the Leopard Woman

I was particularly pleased to speak to the much respected publisher and editor Christopher Sinclair-Stevenson, who was something of a triple threat where Simenon was concerned: he had published him, translated him, and visited him in France (as well as hosting his visits to the UK). Christopher was – characteristically – frank regarding his memories of the author.

'When I was at Hamish Hamilton,' he told me, 'the decision

was made to republish Georges Simenon. It was, in fact, the writer Piers Paul Read's father who had made the suggestion. There had been some translations in the UK, but they had not been published with any enthusiasm or care. I was pleased to take up the cudgels, and I was largely left to my own devices – in fact, I was given no instructions at all! I'd read modern languages at Cambridge, and that was clearly qualification enough to publish this prolific Belgian author.

'Editing and publishing the books should not, theoretically, have been a major task – except that there were so damned many of them. Simenon kept up that amazing flow of work right until the end of his life, but the sheer volume was only part of my problem. There was a certain requirement that was put in place which became known as the "Simenon Rules". These were not generated by Simenon himself, but by his formidable wife Denyse. She Who Must Be Obeyed made it clear to us – in no uncertain terms – that the translations had to be rendered in English that was exactly the equivalent of the French originals. If I suggested that such a thing was not possible – as any translator will tell you, so much of the job is simply a judgement call as to what is the best approximation in another language – it was met with a frosty response, and this became a major challenge of rendering Simenon into English. We quickly learned that there was no profit in arguing with her, and she was known in our offices as the Leopard Woman, principally because she cultivated these long scarlet nails. Of course, it's not unusual for an author to hand the difficult jobs of dealing with a publisher to their spouse, who will then make all the draconian complaints, but I'm not sure whether it was him or her that generated these strict edicts.'

I asked Christopher if his impressions of the author were favourable when meeting him. 'Well,' he replied, 'I can't say that I was greatly enamoured of him in our various encounters. An immensely talented man, of course, but not what I'd call a nice man. My colleague Richard Cobb and I always referred to him as "Le Maître". But we knew we had to tread carefully regarding such issues as translations, as I mentioned earlier. Retrospectively, I suppose it was surprising that I opted to translate Simenon myself – specifically his novel *The Neighbours* (*Le Déménagement*), which was a very bleak piece. But I always admired his non-Maigret novels such as *The Man Who Watched the Trains Go By* (which was, of course, very successfully filmed). I suppose I got to know him personally best when I visited him in Switzerland. There was a ritual dinner which one had to undergo – largely enjoyable, but with its negative side. There were things I would have to put up with… whether I wanted to or not…'

Christopher hesitated, but I insisted that – after this tempting morsel – he had to expand. He laughed and continued. 'All right, it was the women. I had to listen at length to the latest in the continuing series of conquests. My job? Simple… listen and nod admiringly at intervals. As the evening wore on and the Calvados flowed freely, he became even franker and I also had to hear the various prejudices that exercised him – everything you would expect, including homophobia. Happily, though, I didn't have to listen to the usual author complaints about how he was being published in Britain; he was happy with that side of things – happier than his wife, it seemed. Although, interestingly enough, the sales were never strong, although they bubbled over. I think the problem was that he was so damned prolific – I know there were people who assiduously collected every book, but casual readers were never quite sure whether they'd bought a particular Maigret or not. The sales, however, spiked with the television adaptations, which raised the profile of the books.

'I do have one strange memory of what I think was my final visit to the house in Lausanne. We drank, we talked, and all was companionable – but I was particularly aware that the house seemed ever more like a clinic rather than a comfortable residence. And that, in fact, was what it was. His wife Denyse had begun to show – shall we say – peculiarities? And the house was being prepared for when more medically oriented facilities would be required. It was all very strange – in fact, it was more like a subject for a Simenon novel... A house turning into a sinister clinic. It would have to be sinister in a novel, wouldn't it?'

MAIGRET'S PARIS

Simenon places Maigret's office at 36 Quai des Orfèvres, the headquarters of the Parisian judicial police at the Grande Maison, on the banks of the Seine on the Île de la Cité – a place of pilgrimage for the Simenon enthusiast. Venturing inside the building, it is still possible to see the famous 148 steps that Maigret ascended to his office. The cast iron stove and worn linoleum that Simenon described are not to be found, but looking through the windows one can see the boats that Maigret gazed upon, still moving slowly down the Seine.

Rue de Douai to Les Gobelins

The Man Who Watched the Trains Go By/L'Homme qui Regardait Passer les Trains (1938) is virtually a travelogue of Paris, as the protagonist wanders aimlessly around from district to district, sleeping with (but not having sex with) a variety of prostitutes. The novel contains an evocative – and very Parisian – image of an elderly woman selling flowers in the Rue de Douai (an image not impossible to conjure up in modern-day Paris), but it also features a vividly rendered trip to a neighbourhood at the opposite end of town – Les Gobelins – which Maigret finds one of the 'saddest sections of Paris', with wide avenues of depressing flats laid out like army barracks and cafés crowded with 'mediocre people' who are neither rich nor poor.

Pigalle's Prostitutes and the Gare de l'Est

Maigret, in 1934, was originally planned as the last Maigret novel; by this point Simenon had written six novels in a more 'literary' style. In many books, the Pigalle district is where Maigret encounters denizens of the underworld, drug addicts, pimps and prostitutes; and, as described by Simenon, this is a sleazy but curiously attractive area – in fact, it might be said to have been a better class of sleaze in that era, as more downmarket and more sordid distractions have replaced those that Simenon wrote about. Prostitutes still haunt the red light bars, but they seem very unlike those described in the Maigret novels. Similarly, Rue Saint-Denis is much more a tourist hotspot in the twenty-first century than the exotic and atmospheric locale described by Simenon.

Simenon was not above being playful with the conventions of the detective novel – and the identity of the author. In *Maigret's Memoirs/Les Mémoires de Maigret* (1950), Maigret talks about meeting a strange young man called 'Georges Sim' – not hard to guess who this is – who arrives to study him and his working methods, reproducing them Watson-like, with embellishments, in a series of books. Like Holmes, Maigret ruefully remarks on these embellishments and laments their inaccuracy.

The book features the Gare de l'Est, a location familiar to many visitors and one that always evokes scenes of mobilisation for war for the detective. In contrast, Maigret notes, the Gare de Lyon and the Gare Montparnasse always make him think of people going away on holiday – while the Gare du Nord, the gateway to the industrial and mining regions, prompts thoughts of the harsh struggle people once had for their daily bread.

Maigret in Montmartre and the Bois de Boulogne

Maigret at Picratt's/Maigret au Picratt's featured the detective reminiscing about a striptease in Picratt's nightspot in Montmartre. He remembers the stripper wriggling out of her dress with nothing underneath and standing there 'as naked as a worm' – and, as in the American burlesque, 'the moment she has nothing left on all the lights go out'. The sort of discreet strip act that Simenon described here seems quaintly historical now. One has to travel to Montmartre at very specific times of the day to avoid its tourist trap atmosphere today, but it is not impossible to mentally recapture the world Simenon evokes.

Simenon aficionados should be particularly pleased with *Maigret and the Lazy Burglar/Maigret et le Voleur Paresseux* (1961), in which Maigret must disobey orders in order to investigate the murder of an unlikely gang member, whose battered corpse is found in the Bois de Boulogne. The novel is a classic example of Simenon's skill at devising ingenious plots and situations. It features the Palais de Justice (the law court), which is next to the Conciergerie on Île de la Cité at the south corner of Pont au Change. The Conciergerie, which is now a museum, was used as a prison during the French Revolution and was much feared. Prisoners here included Thomas Paine and Mary Antoinette.

From the Bastille to Place des Vosges

The Boulevard Richard-Lenoir figures in *Maigret's Dead Man/Maigret et Son Mort* (1948), in which the detective speculates on the reason for the area's bad reputation. He talks about its unfortunate proximity to the Bastille (hardly a disincentive for the Parisian visitor these days, of course) and, he continues, the area is surrounded by 'miserable slummy little streets'. Again, this is not quite as true of the district in the twenty-first century. Maigret notes, however, the friendly atmosphere and the fact that those who live here grow to love it.

Much of Simenon's Paris has changed since his day, but the beautiful Place des Vosges, however, where Simenon lived, is still very much the area that Simenon evoked, in terms of both its elegant atmosphere and its beauty. At one time, Simenon located his detective's own home here, although Maigret is more often described as living in the Boulevard Richard-Lenoir. The upmarket art galleries and haute cuisine restaurants still nestle under the historic arches, and – more than in many Parisian locations – it is possible to imagine oneself retracing the footsteps of the author's pipe-smoking copper. In addition to Maigret and his prolific creator, famous inhabitants of the square have included Victor Hugo and Théophile Gautier.

One striking memory of Simenon may be found at a watering hole close to the Quai des Orfèvres, the Taverne Henri IV (13 Place du Pont Neuf); the owner was, in fact, a friend of the author, and various photographs on the wall show Simenon enjoying himself at this very location.

Throughout the Maigret novels, the visual aspects of the scene are conveyed impeccably, especially the locations. Simenon's sharp eye for detail is also clearly apparent in his photographic work – as is evidenced by the recent publication of his photographs in *The Years with a Leica* (with a perceptive introduction by the author William Boyd).

More Maigret's Paris

I'm not the only traveller who has savoured the City of Lights with Maigret in mind. The writer Andrew Martin, creator of the evocative Jim Stringer Railway Detective novels (and much else), is a fellow flâneur.

'Paris was always my favourite city,' Andrew says. 'But I couldn't put my finger on why. Then I started to read the Maigret novels of Georges Simenon, and found encapsulated the dreamy, wintry not-trying-too-hard Paris that I loved: zinc-topped bars, blue-jawed toughs drinking from dainty wine glasses, Pont Neuf in the rain, that pre-dinner hour when the lights come on, when everyone is mellow yet galvanised.

'Simenon hated the word "literature", but his psychological understanding and sense of place ensured he was rated by many highbrows. The English traveller aiming to "do" Maigret in a day can begin their appreciation by arriving at the Gare du Nord, described in *Maigret's Memoirs/Les Mémoires de Maigret* as "the coldest, draftiest and busiest" of Paris's stations. "In the morning, the first night trains from Belgium and Germany generally contain a few smugglers, a few traffickers, their faces as hard as the daylight seen through the windows."

'Taking a metro to the heart of Maigret country, you find the police headquarters at 36 Quai des Orfèvres on the Île de la Cité. This is alongside the now-damaged Notre Dame cathedral, but the true Maigret aficionado would be more interested in the nearby restaurants. In *Maigret and the Informer/ Maigret et l'Indicateur* (among others), Maigret lunches at the Brasserie Dauphine, supposedly on the Rue de Harlay, where he favoured the corner table commanding a view of the river.

'The Brasserie Dauphine is thought to have been based on a real-life restaurant in the same spot called the Trois Marches, but in a rare lapse by the planners of central Paris, it has been knocked down and replaced by a bank resembling a Barratt home.

'I visited a restaurant at 13 Place du Pont Neuf, the Taverne Henri IV, where the proprietor, a M. Cointepas, told me that he had been to visit his old customer Simenon in Switzerland shortly before he died in 1989. "He was in a wheelchair, and he couldn't speak... But he was drinking a beer and smoking a pipe," he added. M. Cointepas told me that he often retraces the steps taken by Maigret in his investigations, and at home prepares the dishes described in the books as being favoured by the detective, especially *blanquette de veau* – approximately veal stew. At the time I visited, many senior law enforcers still came into the Taverne at lunchtime – they stood at the bar while the judges sat at the tables. But French detectives no longer drink alcohol during the working day.

'Walking from the Taverne, I arrived at the Place des Vosges in the Fourth Arrondissement. It is surrounded on all four sides by the seventeenth-century buildings that once formed the palace. Incredibly, these fairy-tale premises served – in the 1930s and 1940s – as apartments for the not very well off, including the young Simenon, who set *The Shadow Puppet/L'Ombre Chinoise* here, invoking a world of pinched, disappointed people inhabiting gaslit labyrinths. The building now houses apartments for the wealthy, or baronial antique shops, and Ma Bourgogne at 19 Place des Vosges, depicted in *Madame Maigret's Friend/L'Amie de Madame Maigret* as a dowdy tabac, had become a sumptuous café/

restaurant where *steak frites* were particularly pricey.

'As dusk fell on my Maigret odyssey, I headed for Montmartre, especially the compellingly sleazy vicinity of Boulevard de Clichy. In *Maigret's Memoirs/Les Mémoires de Maigret*, Simenon wrote "the prostitute on Boulevard de Clichy and the inspector watching her both have bad shoes and aching feet after walking up and down kilometres of pavement". In *The Shadow Puppet/L'Ombre Chinoise*, a girl works as a nude dancer at the Moulin Bleu, which is of course based on the Moulin Rouge, the world's most famous strip joint, on Boulevard de Clichy. Simenon once described its wide, dark entrance patrolled by tough-looking men in overcoats, as like "the open maw of a monster".

'There is much red light activity in the Maigret novels, and to sample (or perhaps, we should say, observe) the real-life equivalent, one could walk down the Rue Fontaine and peak at the half-clothed women in the small cave-like bars. This street is the haunt of the murdered pimp, Maurice Marcia, in *Maigret and the Informer/Maigret et l'Indicateur*.

'And to complete my expedition, there was only one option: La Coupole at 102 Boulevard du Montparnasse – not so much because of Maigret, but because of his creator Simenon, who frequented the place in his earlier years, when he was starting work at four in the morning and conducting an affair in the evenings with that exotic temptress and cabaret star Josephine Baker, whom he described as having "the most famous bottom in the world".'

WRITERS ON SIMENON

A Critic's View

One of my happiest associations as a freelance writer for hire was with the then literary editor of the *Independent* newspaper, Boyd Tonkin. It was an association I particularly enjoyed, as Boyd appeared to trust me and very rarely tweaked my reviews before they appeared in the paper. And as – without trying – I had become something of a specialist in crime in translation, I'd put myself in the firing line where Boyd was concerned, as that was very much his area – and remains so. He reminded me recently that he had written about Simenon for *The Times*, and told me, 'Simenon's also in my *100 Best Novels in Translation* book – after much deliberation, I chose *The Snow Was Dirty*, though several others would have done as well.'

'Inspector Maigret's last case, *Maigret and Monsieur Charles/ Maigret et Monsieur Charles* (recently translated by Ros Schwartz), ends not with guilt and remorse but with a murderer who "appeared to be very much at ease". And why not? For the woman who slew a philandering high-society lawyer has finally had the privilege of encountering the clumsy provincial detective who looks into the souls of the wrongdoers he hunts and grants them a kind of absolution. *Maigret and Monsieur Charles*, which Georges Simenon finished in February 1972, bookends the series of 75 Maigret novels that began, in 1931, with *Pietr the Latvian/Pietr-le-Letton*. Simenon, though, had no deep-laid plans to do away with his fictional chief of the Paris crime squad. On 18 September 1972, he sat down to plan a new non-Maigret novel — *Victor* — with his usual ritual of sketching outlines on a manila envelope. Nothing came. He abandoned the idea, and then his phenomenal career in fiction. "I no longer needed to put myself in the skin of everyone I met," his memoirs record. "I was free at last."

'The Liège-born Simenon never went in for half-measures. The 75 Maigret mysteries (although Simenon's hawk-eyed biographer Patrick Marnham tallies them at 76) stand alongside 117 "serious" novels, mostly psychological thrillers in the deepest shades of *noir*, and the 200-odd pulp potboilers of his torrentially productive youth. Then, of course, there are the 10,000 women he once claimed (in an interview with his chum Federico Fellini) to have slept with [as mentioned earlier]; his second wife later revised the estimate down to 1,200. Beyond dispute, his books had sold over 500 million copies by his death in 1989.

'Maigret was born in 1929, in the Dutch port of Delfzijl, on Simenon's boat the *Ostrogoth*. The Belgian author began to imagine a burly detective, "a big man who ate a lot, drank a lot, followed the suspects patiently and eventually uncovered the truth". Over the next four decades, as he moved from Paris to western France, Canada, New York, Florida, Arizona, the Côte d'Azur and Switzerland, his bondage to Maigret yielded not just the world's bestselling detective series but an imperishable literary legend. Slow, placid, bulky, pipe-chomping, hatted, overcoated (even on the sun-kissed Riviera), the inspector does not so much chase clues as decipher tormented minds. An anti-Sherlock Holmes, he exposes secrets, lies and crimes not by forensic wizardry but through the melded powers of therapist, philosopher — and confessor. Maigret mooches from bar to bar, workshop to workshop, flat to flat, as if absorbing evidence from the very stones, tastes and smells of Paris.

'Jules Maigret first wanted to study medicine. But a flashback novel, *Maigret's First Case/La Première Enquête de Maigret* (1949), returns to his early police career. Young Jules longs to be "a cross between a doctor and a priest" — "a sort of mender of destinies". Which he duly becomes. The truth, via its thickset, smoke-wreathed emissary, will set his anguished quarries free. This Belgian immigrant's ideal of French reason and insight never judges. He observes, connects and understands.

'Although 1930s Maigrets range widely, around provincial France and into the Low Countries, later volumes tend to stick to central Paris. From the Police Judiciare HQ on the Quai des Orfèvres to the modest flat on Boulevard Richard-Lenoir the inspector shares with his ever attentive wife, by way of village-like Montmartre, gritty Canal Saint-Martin and the swanky streets around the Champs-Élysées, Simenon turns Paris into a landscape of myth. He hardly lived in the city after 1932. So Maigret's beloved *quartiers* become — for all their seedy, whiffy plausibility — imaginary heartlands, like Narnia or The Shire. The hearty bistro *plats*, the sticky old liqueurs, the flash southern mobsters: all speak of a vanished Paris. When, in late Maigrets, we come across miniskirts and discos, it's as if Poirot had whipped out an iPhone.

'Together, the Maigrets add up to a huge, utterly coherent inventory of lust, fear, greed, ambition, jealousy and long-hidden pain, brought to light by an implacably curious mind. Simenon's slimmed-down vocabulary (2,000 words or so) adds to their taut intensity. He called them "semi-literary" works and wished to be judged for his darkly brilliant *romans durs* ("tough novels"). But André Gide – one of Simenon's countless literary devotees – meant Maigret too when he lauded the Belgian as "the greatest of all, the most genuine novelist we have had". Penguin's now complete shelf of gem-hard soul-probes should allow a new generation to understand why.'

The Art of Simenon

A favourite writer of mine – the French crime novelist Thomas Narcejac – provided some valuable insights into a writer who had inspired him in *The Art of Simenon*. And Narcejac himself was an interesting figure – although most people only knew his surname as part of the portmanteau Boileau–Narcejac. The prolific and ingenious French writing duo produced the original novel on which Henri-Georges Clouzot's film *Les Diaboliques* was based; they wrote another ingeniously plotted book, *D'Entre les Morts/From Among the Dead/The Living and the Dead* (1954), which provided the basis for one of Hitchcock's supreme masterpieces, *Vertigo* (1958). Their influence on crime fiction – principally through the films made of their work – continues to this day, but this immensely professional duo of Gallic scribes also wrote intelligent critical essays on the genre, such as Narcejac's Simenon study.

According to Narcejac, 'Simenon never tries to fox his readers or lay traps for them like the writers of the classic detective stories. He despises the enigma of the locked room; he dislikes alibis and logical impediments. The complex mechanisms of the detective story leave him cold. He is not interested in the "how" but the "why". He does not even pay particular attention to the logical sequence of episodes, to the preparation of the little detail, the tiny cog in the wheel which is always the turning point of the true detective story. For instance, in *Night at the Crossroads/La Nuit du Carrefour*, we find Maigret looking everywhere for the revolver which he had previously put in his pocket. In *A Crime in Holland/Un Crime en Hollande*, the detective gets himself arrested by the Dutch police, and is put in prison. A little later, after having been searched in the routine manner, he pretends to shoot himself in the middle of an interrogation in order to put journalists off the scent. It seems highly improbable that any journalist would take such an astonishing development quite seriously. Incidentally, in Simenon's first books, it is obvious that Simenon is at a loss when he has to formulate a real problem in detection. He finds the logic of events tedious, since they are opposed to the logic of feeling. Simenon is, admittedly, not incapable of inventing an exciting mystery, provided that it springs from character, and this seems to me a vital point. For according to Simenon, the mystery is never the result of a voluntary deception on the part of the criminal, and the policeman has never to compete in ingenuity with him. On the contrary, the criminal is naive: he kills because he cannot do otherwise, and he never dreams of making his crime ridiculous by careful staging. The policeman, whether he be Maigret, the Little Doctor or Inspector Torrence, does not need to be a genius. All he has to do is to understand or, better still, *feel* the psychological significance of his clues, and not their material significance.

'This is a far cry from the detective story. Even the choice of clues is peculiar. Simenon never loads his narrative with hairs, specks of mud or dust or bloodstains. He never tries to find out whether the murderer came in here and went out there. He never questions witnesses to find out the exact time and the smallest details of the crime. A clue, to him, is something much vaguer and more rewarding: a gesture, a word, a glance. There is only one question the reader need ask: "If I had committed this crime, would I have made that gesture, spoken that word, cast that glance?" This approach takes it for granted that the crime might have been committed by the reader – that is to say, by any normal man, victim of a universal passion, one of those from which we have all, on occasion, suffered. Thus, to resolve the mystery is not, for Simenon, to discover the criminal's method, but purely and simply to experience, as it were, to relive the psychological crisis which provoked the drama. The reader should sympathise with the murderer, who is never a monster, but just a poor, unhappy bastard.

'Thus Simenon can easily dispense with the dramatic surprises, the sensational discoveries and unexpected revelations which must necessarily characterise the classic detective story. Instead of pursuing a phantom murderer through 250 pages, he reveals the criminal little by little, gently bringing us to admit the psychological necessity of his act. As we discover the truth, we excuse the man who has killed, or more precisely, we take pity on him. One might perhaps even say that we understand in so far as we take pity. For Simenon knows two forms of truth. The one is as dry, formal and purely objective as a police court or a legal deposition. It ignores motives and is solely related to facts. It is icily inhuman, scientific and false, as radically false as any explanation which purports to explain the whole of life. The other truth is lived, it is inward and incommunicable, the truth of secrecy and the confessional. It despises logic, intelligence and the sense of geometry. It is a truth of the soul, which is alien to proof or demonstration. It is the truth of feeling. But you must be very much alive and young of heart to perceive it. The successful, those who have silenced their secret longing for integrity and authenticity, either through ambition, avarice or pride, these only know a fabricated truth. They are on the side of the judges and the hangman. Madame Monde is talking to the police about her husband's disappearance: "All that she had told the inspector had been true, but it sometimes happens that there is no bigger falsehood than the truth." And speaking of Monsieur Monde, Simenon adds, later, "He was certainly not disincarnate. He was still M. Monde, or Desire, certainly Desire... It did not matter. He was a man who had borne with his human condition for a long time without being aware of it, just like those who do not know that they are ill. He had been a man amongst men... And now, suddenly, he saw life differently, as if under an ultra-powerful X-ray. All that had previously been important, the outer envelope, the flesh and sinew, existed no more, nor false appearances, nor practically anything, and in their place... but there you were, it was not worth mentioning. Besides, it wasn't possible. It was not communicable."

'The secret of being. The mystery of our actions, of our thoughts, of our destiny, all rooted in that subterranean region of the self into which reflection does not penetrate.

'Simenon created Maigret primarily in order to try to reach the inner nature of his characters through this privileged personage. Maigret a detective? Not a bit. Maigret is above all a man. Simenon has given him a very special quality of solidity, consistency and density. You need to be of strong bone and muscle to experience all the impulses that trouble our weak flesh and our unhappy human consciences. Maigret is, first of all, capable of feeling everything. Simenon has given him a finesse which is almost an instinct, which makes him able to perceive and interpret the faint emanations which arise imperceptibly from places and persons, for places have also their hidden significance, their dim awareness, their primitive mentalities, just like human beings. Man is plunged into his environment (town, suburb, village, isolated house) like a fish into water, and there is an uninterrupted interaction between the person and his habitat. Simenon's criminals are often men who have not found their proper climate, hence the disequilibrium, the crisis, the explosion of violence. It is Maigret's task, not to explain the criminal, but as it were to take charge of him, and in a mysterious way, assume his burden. Since crime is usually the result of a lack of vitality, Maigret acts rather like a blood donor. He infuses the warmth and life that is lacking to a sick environment. His very presence modifies the quality of the other characters. They are tranquillised and relax, become once more normal individuals, and as they are transformed, their crime becomes detached from them and loses its heaviness and bestiality. Without saying a word, Maigret is able to absorb the negative emanations and neutralise them. Finally the murderer can talk about his crime. He feels that Maigret has also committed it, has lived it, mimed it and blotted it out. Between man and man there may be a confession. Thanks to Maigret the murderer is not cut off from the human communion. His fault remains sin, but calls for pardon. Maigret is much less a detective than a "weigher of souls". The investigations, the questionings, the shadowings are of no importance, as is shown by the fact that the novels without Maigret are constructed on exactly the same lines as the novels with Maigret. There is no essential difference between *The Hanged Man of Saint-Pholien/Le Pendu de Saint-Pholien* and *The Strangers in the House/Les Inconnus dans la Maison*. The first is only a faint sketch of the second. The lawyer Loursat is to deputise for Maigret. But Simenon's technique is identical in both. His way of attacking the story and of slowly revealing his characters has not undergone any significant modification. "Ascent towards the novel," as Sigaux says? Surely the pure novel has been there from the very beginning. The most one might concede is that one day Simenon was to perceive that Maigret was not necessary. Why should not the principal character be his own witness? Why should not Maigret's tenacious investigations be undertaken by the man who is one day driven to distraction by the pressure of circumstance, and tries to discover the secret of his own life, of his own heart? Donge, Monde, the hero of *Act of Passion/Lettre à Mon Juge*, Malétras, Loursat, Bergelon and many another are Maigret all over again, in so far as their self-respect compels them to observe and judge with lucidity the evil that obsesses them.'

The Authentic Simenon

For the academic publisher Intellect, I edited a book in their 'Crime Uncovered' series called *Detective*, which was designed as a celebration of a variety of iconic sleuths. I was in the enviable position of being able to choose those I wished to cover myself before assigning essays to other writers, but as I was planning to tackle Colin Dexter's Inspector Morse and Henning Mankell's Kurt Wallander, I decided to place Jules Maigret in the capable hands of Jonathan Wilkins, author of the Utrecht trilogy. His excellent piece — while notably more dyspeptic than other entries in the volume — was full of keen and original insights, particularly concerning the contrast between Simenon's Maigret novels and his *romans durs*.

'I believe that we can see the true, authentic Georges Simenon in Jules Maigret,' Wilkins noted. 'The chief inspector is the man his creator wished to be. Simenon may have believed his non-Maigret novels were to be his principal life's work, but after failing to win the Nobel Prize, he retreated into the world of his policeman, who personifies that which Simenon himself could never be. The author lived in the world of his *romans durs* (or "hard novels"), and while we see his dark and calculating side, in Maigret we see the man... It is not often that we gaze into the soul of Maigret, and when we are permitted to do so it is both intriguing and enlightening. He is a rare sort of man, a hero who does not recognise himself as such. A quotidian figure at one with the victim, but also with the perpetrator. He sympathises with both. We believe in Maigret, as he is one of us. He believes in us; he is on our side. In the comforting, tobacco-scented presence of Inspector Maigret, we are comforted. Who would not want to believe in a man like that, serene and reassuring?

'Critics have discerned two key aspects of Simenon's work: tragedy and wisdom. The wisdom shines forth in the Maigret stories, where the stark motifs of tragedy, subjected to the uncompromising glare of Simenon's artistry, come under the softening influence of the detective's humanity.

'Hilary Mantel talks of writing with '"maximum ambiguity"', and we can see this in the two shades of Simenon. It is apparent in *The Snow Was Dirty*, another of his self-proclaimed *romans durs*. Often thought to be based in an unnamed city of France or in Brussels, Simenon insisted the book was set in an Eastern European state. The ambiguity is typical of the author in the avoidance of any political reference to France, his adopted nation, though we can extrapolate. The novel was written in 1948, and is another of the books Simenon hoped might win him the Nobel Prize for Literature. The story is set in a town under occupation, though Simenon was insistent that the setting was not occupied France. Why did he want to disguise the setting? The author – by not identifying the country – is perhaps attempting to universalise the narrative, which centres on the amoral and cynical 19-year-old Frank Friedmaier in a winter of endless snow that serves a symbolic function throughout the novel. In the opening scene Frank stabs an enemy soldier as he walks home through the snow at night. The murder is nothing to do with any act of rebellion against the occupier or of patriotism. It is a pointlessly evil act that Frank describes as "losing his virginity"... The novel is revealing concerning Simenon and his perhaps nihilistic world view, radically different here from his Maigret novels, suggesting the work of two different writers: the self-styled "typewriter" who rushes out his detective stories with such speed and the aspiring Nobel Prize winner. His attitude to literary acclaim and popular success was complex: Simenon proclaimed that he would write a novel in a glass box as a publicity stunt, and was ridiculed by the elitist writers of the day. He never felt that he was given his due, and perhaps he was right. But he was partly responsible for such attitudes.'

PUBLISHING SIMENON
IN THE MODERN AGE

Sitting in Soho with Simenon's Son

There are definite perks to being a writer of books on crime fiction, such as an invitation in 2013 to a meal at discreet Soho House (situated, coincidentally, in Soho) with Georges Simenon's son, who bears the Anglo-Saxon first name 'John' rather than the expected 'Jean'. The occasion was the inaugural dinner for the newly convened Simenon society – which was also, in fact, the launch of Penguin's ambitious programme of reissuing all 75 Maigret novels in spanking new translations (the first being *Pietr the Latvian*, translated by David Bellos). The appearance of this inaugural book – and the meal itself – was very timely, as I had just written the Simenon chapter of *Euro Noir* and I had just described that first novel as *The Case of Peter the Lett* – which was how it was previously translated in the UK. The editor of the new series (and host for the evening), Josephine Greywoode, said that Penguin were attempting to get closer to Maigret's originals than in previous translations – which was certainly the case with the book's title. And translation was very much a theme of the evening, as one of the finest practitioners of that art in the UK, Siân Reynolds, was present (she has rendered into English several later books in the series). She told us about the challenges of working in French with such heirs of Simenon as Fred Vargas – although, apparently, the latter does not consider herself as such.

Guests included *The Sunday Times*' Andrew Holgate and über-agent Caroline Michel, but the star of the evening was John Simenon, who turned out to be urbane, knowledgeable and highly agreeable company. What's more, over the *moules* and *boeuf au vin rouge*, Simenon *fils* was more than happy to talk at length about his famous father – even though his own career as a film distributor is equally interesting (he mentioned how he had had some difficulty selling in Europe two then little-known films, *Rocky* and *One Flew Over the Cuckoo's Nest*). We heard about Georges Simenon's thoroughly practical view of his craft; his admiration for the great Russian writers such as Dostoevsky (and his immersion in the philosophy of Nietzsche); and his views of actors who had played his pipe-smoking detective, such as Rupert Davies – who Simenon described as his 'perfect Maigret' – and those who had actually spoken the correct language, such as Jean Gabin.

We all tiptoed around the subject of the claim Simenon made about the number of women he had slept with, but his son brought it up himself, hinting that we should not take Simenon *père* at his word. 'One of the things my father was particularly good at – *avant la lettre* – was publicity and promotion. Such as making provocative remarks about his prodigious number of sexual experiences. Well, it worked, didn't it? Here we are still talking about it around a dinner table in 2013!'

But we were really there to celebrate the astonishing achievement of Georges Simenon, the favourite crime writer of so many crime writers. I told his son that I planned to read every one of the novels sequentially, something I had never done before – if, that is, I live long enough. I still haven't finished them all…

Penguin and Simenon

As mentioned above, in 2013 Penguin Classics UK began an ambitious programme under the stewardship of editor Josephine Greywoode to issue all 75 Maigret novels in new translations. In 2022, the programme was completed. Speaking to Josephine, I asked her how the project came to her – did she decide that it was time for new versions of all the Maigret novels?

'No, in fact it happened because of the Maigret estate,' she replied. 'They were the instigators. They came to Penguin and said, "We have managed to get all the rights more or less into the same place – do you have a proposal as to what you could do with them?" For Penguin Classics, this was a really exciting invitation. I knew that in the past these books had been published as genre fiction, but they had never been given the classic treatment – so when we thought about what we could do, the notion of new modern translations came to the fore. How could we do this differently? All the books had appeared in English before, but what could we do that would be a bit more ambitious – a move that would make it worthwhile? Penguin had published several tranches before – say, ten books here, ten books there, but we considered that a really ambitious notion would be to make it into a full-scale translation project that would tackle the reader's experience in English versions – something that had previously been patchy. Some translations had been good, some less so, and some departed markedly from the originals – as Simenon found out himself in his lifetime. We knew that Adelphi had done something like this in Milan; over a longer period of time, they had created a space for this author in the cultural sphere in Italy that we could see as possible in other markets. That was the inspiration: a serious literary publisher who elevated an author's work. The idea was to make everyone treat Simenon as the great writer he was rather than just as an entertaining genre specialist.'

Nowadays, I suggested, Simenon was taken much more seriously; did they consider the success of their project to be part of that trend?

Josephine chuckled. 'I wish we could take credit for that,' she said, 'but, to be frank, I wasn't greatly familiar with him when we started — although language is a speciality of mine (French, Italian), which made me a good fit to spearhead this project, particularly the translation aspect of it. The depth and the richness of his output was something of a discovery for me. It was very daunting for me at the start, I must admit — this huge, huge project, 30,000 to 40,000 words in each of the books. My God! I remember that Simenon was asked at some point when he was going to write his "big novel", and he replied that he was doing so — his big novel was the sum of all his books. Reading all the books, you get this complex web — the nuances, the way he builds particular themes, the way he tackles different social issues, his world view, his curiosity.'

I mentioned to Josephine the problems that Christopher Sinclair-Stevenson had described to me about the Simenon translation process in his day. I imagined now that the only real interventions would come from her?

'Well,' she replied, 'you'd have to ask the translators how

interventionist they considered me to be! There was one way that we circumvented a lot of problems. The translator Ros Schwartz had a brilliant idea – she suggested that we get all the translators together. David Bellos had translated the first book in our series, and we were able to put together something of a style sheet, so that we could really try to create a consistency for the reader. This might have been something of a straitjacket for translators who wanted to come up with their own creative solutions, but we did want readers to think they were returning to the same world. We tried to avoid a jolt between books; Simenon's voice was what counted. And Ros's suggestion – that we all get together – took place, I'm glad to say. We all went, fittingly enough, to a château in Belgium – and we thrashed out many problems. It was a highly unusual initiative for some of the translators, who were much more used to working on their own. The guiding principle, of course, remained to keep the new books as faithful as possible to the originals. And, as I'm sure you know, Barry, there are inconsistencies of plot in Simenon – something that came up again and again. I would always say to the translators: "Let's keep it in – after all, if you were a French reader you'd notice it. So let's not iron out those imperfections." He didn't – as part of his process – go through rigorously straightening these things out, did he?'

I mentioned Christopher Sinclair-Stevenson's remarks to me about Simenon's insistence that the translations be as close to the originals as possible. Did Josephine consider that feasible, given the individual voices the translators would have?

'You're right,' she replied, 'if you're suggesting that it's not really feasible – and you wouldn't want to alter the individual voice of a translator, even though, of course, they must be at the service of the original text. And it's crucial that a translation remains close to the rhythm of Simenon's prose, which is quite unusual. The syntax and sentence structure of the original is, of course, un-English, but it would be a mistake to smooth it out too much. For instance, we had a long conversation at that meeting in Belgium about all the ellipses. Several of the translators said, "Oh, there are so many ellipses – can we get rid of some?" So there is a judgement call there. We tried to keep as many as we could, but inevitably you had to render the text into the best possible English.'

I mentioned the response I had had from somebody who had read only one book, which didn't really register with them – and my reply that you need to have read a whole tranche to get the true Simenon flavour. Did she agree?

'Absolutely! In fact, a colleague of mine in publishing said exactly that to me recently. They tried one or two but only when they read a whole batch of them did they become totally attuned – and they now consider themselves addicted! But we've been utterly relentless in positioning him as a great writer. And as for the snobbery that is sometimes directed at the crime genre – well, I hope we have proved how ridiculous that is with our project.'

I suggested to Josephine that many readers nowadays – in the twenty-first century – look at fiction of the past through a prism of what is now acceptable, and Simenon admirers are well aware that there are aspects of his books that are not consonant with increasingly rigid views.

'Oh, there were certainly discussions on this issue,' Josephine replied. 'After all, these books were written in the

1930s and often reflect attitudes that were prevalent then. That's the case even with some of the subsequent ones. And what was part of the culture back then – well, it doesn't go down so well these days, does it?'

In such cases, did Josephine say to her translators, 'Let's go with it,' or would she attempt – without censoring the text – to soften the blow?

'The latter! Because the whole ethos of the project was to be as faithful as possible to Simenon, there was no way we could simply erase these difficult views. Without censoring, we would try to avoid something that would, well, shall we say, disorient the modern reader. When you're confronted with what might be perhaps outdated views about certain ethnic groups, that would have had a different effect on the modern reader than at the time, well, that's just the water you are swimming in. That was the balance – not to bowdlerise or censor the books, but – as you said – to slightly soften it. After all, we don't read them as one would read Zola or Flaubert; Simenon still seems very modern, which is why these tricky sections really leap out as incongruous. So a description, for instance, that a character has a "Semitic appearance" might be somehow changed into something about their Jewish ancestry – the word "Semitic" is not racist, but the context might be uncomfortable.'

So, at the time of writing, is the Simenon project at an end for Josephine and Penguin Classics?

'No – there are still some standalones to come, and I think you've written somewhere, Barry, that some of his best work is in the standalones, so we are keen to publish those. I have reinforcements to help me make selections of those. As you

know, we have translated some of the short stories, but we plan to publish more — some of them are really terrific, and quite as good as the novels. As for the future — well, I'm still doing some translation-related projects, but I think I deserve a breather after something like the massive Simenon project, don't you? I loved the creative challenge, but it was damned hard work keeping it on track, even though I relished doing so.'

So, perhaps it's time to talk to some of the translators Josephine employed...

TRANSLATING SIMENON

The translation issues relating to Denyse Simenon's strictures, as mentioned earlier, might have raised the pulse rates of translators in the past, but the recent versions have utilised the cream of the profession, including David Bellos, the late Anthea Bell, Linda Coverdale, David Coward, Howard Curtis, Will Hobson, Siân Reynolds, Ros Schwartz, David Watson and Shaun Whiteside. I decided to ask several of them about the challenges they faced, and translators – always highly sensitive to their art being undervalued – didn't take a great deal of persuasion to talk about their work on Simenon.

No Glossing Over: Ros Schwartz

Ros Schwartz has translated some 100 works of fiction and non-fiction. In addition to some 20 Simenon titles, she has translated crime fiction by Dominique Manotti and Sébastien Japrisot, a range of writers from the African continent, and fiction for young adults. In 2009, Ros was made a Chevalier dans l'Ordre des Arts et des Lettres; she frequently takes part in literary events and festivals, at several of which I have run into her.

I began by asking her if she found any particular challenges when translating Georges Simenon as opposed to other authors she's worked on.

'Most of the authors I translate are still living,' Ros replied, 'so I'm able to enter into a dialogue with them and ask them for clarifications. Simenon is no longer with us, so that isn't possible. There is a lot of period detail in his descriptions, so part of the job is doing detective work myself to find images of items he refers to – but that's also part of the fun. In one description of a woman sleeping with *épingles* in her hair at night, I eventually found the exact bobby pins... advertised on eBay! My ancient *Harrap's*, which I bought with the money from my paper round when I was 15 and has been languishing on a shelf for the past 35 years, has really come into its own. I found the specific word for the room in a railway station where the oil lamps are stored – *lampisterie*/lamp-room – in there.

'One challenge for me as a middle-aged woman is dealing with Simenon's often sexist comments. An older woman is "good-looking even though she's over 50", and a maid, who we are told is fat and spotty, is always referred to as "the fat, spotty maid". And as for poor Madame Maigret, at Maigret's beck and call at all hours of day and night, and who doesn't need entertaining because she keeps herself busy with her laundry and her cooking... We have strict editorial instructions to translate everything as Simenon wrote it, so no glossing over some of his more offensive descriptions. But he was of his time, and it would be inappropriate to airbrush out that aspect.

'Another challenge is Simenon's punctuation. In some of his books, almost every sentence ends with an exclamation mark or an ellipsis. This requires some consultation with the editors because it looks very odd in English. I declared war on the ellipsis in some of the titles.'

Similarly, I asked, did Ros find any particular rewards in the task?

'It's rare to have the privilege of translating numerous books by the same author. Having "lived" with Simenon for the past eight years (I feel more married to Maigret than poor Madame Maigret!), I have gained insights into what drives his writing. Simenon is intrigued by what motivates an ordinary person to commit a crime — what their tipping point is. It's not about "whodunnit" but "why they dunnit" that fascinates him.

'He is endlessly curious about human nature. Maigret's role is more that of a father confessor than a cop. Very often, he knows who the murderer is — so does the reader — and the murderer knows he knows. The dénouement is the confession. Often, the killer goes free — Maigret's satisfaction is in resolving the mystery rather than seeing the perpetrator behind bars. Simenon is clearly on the side of the little people against the corrupt elites. Maigret will leave no stone unturned to find the murderer of a working-class girl or to expose the skeletons in the cupboards of the wealthy. He is keenly attuned to resentments that build up over a lifetime — deriving from sexual humiliation, abuse in childhood, professional failure — which suddenly surface and drive a person to murder.

'I particularly love Simenon's "killer grannies", the sweet little old lady who turns out to be a ruthless murderer. In fact, many of his women are interesting: sexual predators, women with agency, in an era when women didn't have many options. And when a woman turns to crime, it is often because she has limited life choices: find a wealthy husband or become a prostitute. Simenon is not judgemental — he shows human life in all its infinite variety.'

And, I asked, how many Simenon books has Ros translated? And did she attempt to reflect the ethos and feeling of the book as it would have been received by the first readers, or is the language she used completely contemporary?

'To date, I have translated 16 Maigret titles, two *romans durs* — *Betty* and *The Venice Train* — and a number of short stories. The *romans durs* are dark and deeply disturbing. There are existing translations that were made when the books were first written, and so the point of a new translation is that it needs to be different. Simenon is extraordinarily economical with language, which is surprisingly challenging to replicate. He can paint an entire town in a few simple brushstrokes. If I were to try to describe what I am doing in the translation, I would say I want my reader to see, hear, smell and taste what the French reader sees, hears, smells and tastes. I aim to replicate the atmosphere of the period and am careful not to use anachronisms, while seeking to ensure that the translation is, first and foremost, a good read in English.

'As to Simenon's appeal for a modern readership, I'm not sure that's for me to say! Personally, I find his plots utterly compelling. The books are all short, around 35,000 words, which fits in well with today's lifestyle. The novels vividly evoke Paris and the provincial life of the 1930s to the 1950s, and so have nostalgia appeal. And Simenon deals with human passions — in the same way that Greek tragedy still speaks to us. If I were to advise a new reader of Simenon, I'd say tackle several titles to get a full taste of his work and a sense of the themes running through his novels. And don't read him through the lens of twenty-first-century political correctness — he was of his time. I believe he was fundamentally sympathetic to the difficulties facing women and the disadvantaged classes.'

Time-Specific and Yet Timeless: Howard Curtis

I have known Howard Curtis for decades, and have watched with interest the growth of his reputation as a translator. Howard has translated more than a hundred books from French, Italian and Spanish. Apart from over 20 books by Simenon, the French authors he has translated include Balzac, Flaubert, André Malraux, Georges Bernanos, Jean-Claude Izzo, Yasmina Khadra and Carole Martinez. From Italian, he has translated Pirandello, Leonardo Sciascia, Gianrico Carofiglio, Giorgio Scerbanenco, Marco Malvaldi and many more. From Spanish he has translated, among others, Luis Sepúlveda and Santiago Gamboa. He was the first person I spoke to about translating Simenon, and his comments were pertinent.

'The first thing you need to do, as a translator,' he told me, 'is divest yourself of the idea that Simenon is an easy author to translate. True, he writes in quite a simple style: he deliberately restricted his vocabulary to make it comprehensible to as wide a readership as possible. But along with that simplicity goes an extraordinary concision, an extraordinary precision. Time and again, you come across beautifully turned phrases that sum up a character, a setting, a mood in the minimum of words, and it's often a struggle, for a translator, to find equivalents in English. Translating a writer with a more florid style can, in a way, be easier: you can cheat a little, paraphrase, blur over the finer points, and something will still be there. None of that with Simenon: leave anything out and the whole thing collapses. The challenge, as well as the joy, for a Simenon translator, is to match his concision and precision with a concision and precision of your own.

'Personally, my other great joy is that I'm translating a writer who's been a favourite of mine ever since I first read him, at the age of 13 or so. If I'm going to enter someone else's mind for a few months, which is what a translator has to do, then I'm happy it's Simenon.

'To give an example of what a delicate task translation can be: a few years ago, I translated one of Simenon's finest (if darkest) novels, *The Snow Was Dirty*, a bleak story of a petty criminal in a city under foreign occupation in wartime. Wanting to convey the directness of the style, I used contractions almost throughout: "he's" rather than "he is", "can't" rather than "cannot" (the book is mostly in the present tense). The editors disagreed with me: they thought the important thing to emphasise was the coldness and remoteness of the novel's mood, which meant the contractions had to go. Both approaches were equally valid, I think. In the end, as in all good relationships, we reached a compromise: lots of contractions, but not throughout!

'One of the remarkable things about Simenon is how time-specific and yet how timeless he is. His books offer an incredibly detailed portrait of life in France from the 1930s to the 1970s. (True, he did write about other parts of the world, but most of his novels are set in France.) The streets of Paris, the little provincial towns, the canals, the cafés, the seedy hotels, the gossipy concierges: they are all vividly there. We can almost taste the Calvados that Maigret downs in some Parisian bistro. At the same time, his themes are universal, which is why he's still enjoyable to read today: the reader can simultaneously revel in a kind of nostalgia for a world gone by and identify with characters whose dilemmas are so human and so believable. It's important for the translator to convey both the period flavour and the continuing relevance of the work, treading a fine line between bringing the language up to date and yet not being anachronistic.

'As for where to start with Simenon: among the Maigret novels I'd recommend one that has been a favourite of mine since I first read it in my teens (and had the great luck to translate decades later): *Maigret's Mistake*. This claustrophobic story, with its small number of characters and its typically atmospheric rendering of milieu, perfectly illustrates the mixture of intuition and compassion that has made Maigret such a beloved figure. Among the non-Maigrets, I'd recommend *The Krull House*, a story of xenophobia and mob hysteria, set in a vividly depicted provincial French town in the 1930s: a novel both firmly rooted in its time and place and frighteningly relevant in its theme.'

Undercurrents: Siân Reynolds

I was keen to talk to a key Simenon translator, Siân Reynolds. Siân was born in Cardiff, read languages at Oxford, has a doctorate in history from Paris, and is Emerita Professor of French at the University of Stirling. Alongside her academic career, she has translated the historical works of Fernand Braudel and the fiction of Fred Vargas and Virginie Despentes.

I began by asking her about the challenges and problems she faced.

'When Penguin first approached me about the project of a new translation of Georges Simenon's Maigret novels, two things immediately came to mind. First, I was doubtful about re-translating books that had already been well translated — especially by living translators. This question was eventually resolved by Penguin in various ways, but right away, Josephine Greywoode as commissioning editor was sympathetic and suggested I take a novel either not translated at all, or long out of print. So I began with *A Crime in Holland/Un Crime en Hollande* (1931), a very early title translated by the late Geoffrey Sainsbury, about whom I knew nothing. This turned out to be instructive.

'After I'd sent my own translation in, I apprehensively ordered the Sainsbury version from the library — then wondered if I had been working from the wrong text. His translation was very readable in its way, but departed quite radically from the original, embellishing or cutting it. For instance, he completely changed the last scene — where Maigret gathers the suspects and explains the murder, making it — as he considered — clearer for the reader. John Simenon later told us that Sainsbury had indeed chosen to produce his own versions of "Simenon", as the novelist later discovered. There are many ways to translate a book. At Penguin, the idea behind the whole new series is to try to get as close as we can to the way Simenon wrote.

'This experience was not unrelated to the second thing that occurred to me. I naively assumed that the Maigret novels would not be too hard to translate, because I remembered them as written rather simply and straightforwardly. How wrong I was. They are hard to translate *because* they are written simply. As most people know, Simenon uses a fairly restricted vocabulary. That does not mean that he repeats himself. He doesn't, unless deliberately. He exploits the French language in subtle ways that set the translator problems if they are not going to repeat words a great deal. Thanks to my excellent copyeditor, Claire Peligry, I quickly became aware, for example, how often in English we use many-sided words such as "look" and "back" (it looked like rain, he looked angry, she looked across the room, the look on her face; to come back in, turn your back on, fold back the sheets, etc., etc). That is an example at the superficial level of lexis.

'More seriously – and I know my fellow translators are well aware of this – Simenon's simplicity conceals complexity and undercurrents. He doesn't spell things out. Sainsbury's approach – which did spell things out – made him grate his teeth. By comparison, and strangely enough, when a book is written in a more wide-ranging and detailed way, both in terms of vocabulary and subject matter, it may make it easier to translate. There is some wriggle room, and the translator does not have to squeeze into a confined space. That, at least, is my experience of translating other writers – for example, the enjoyably quirky detective novels of Fred Vargas, which allow you to be quirky in response. Simenon requires discipline, not expansion.

'There are other peculiarities of a Simenon novel that we had to resolve at series level. For example, it might look superficial, but he makes much use of the three dots... – a feature found in other French authors. In Simenon, it is taken to great lengths: it may indicate an unfinished sentence of dialogue, or it may figure in the narrative suggesting that there is more there than meets the eye. It's not common in English, and I remember that when the Penguin translators met up for a fruitful, and enjoyable, weekend near Liège, Simenon's birthplace, we spent a lot of time discussing how to handle it.

'There is also the tricky question of the period and style of language, especially dialogue. Practically all the Maigret novels were written between the 1930s and the 1960s. Some of the social markers and attitudes expressed are inevitably of their time: that includes turns of phrase (usually, but not always, in dialogue – i.e. not the author's voice) which would not be acceptable now. There are examples of what one might characterise as casual anti-Semitism or misogyny or otherwise non-inclusive language, which, to be fair, are found in most other novels of the period. Even the title of one book I translated, *Maigret's Madwoman* (a literal translation of *La Folle de Maigret*), would perhaps not be chosen today. But the series does try, as far as possible, to replicate the original titles. A translator normally has, as a first principle, to be faithful to the text, but I think there are times when all of us have compromised a bit.

'Linguistically, and this is rather surprising, Simenon's dialogue, whoever is speaking, is usually in rather formal – or at any rate *correct* – French, rather than spoken French of the time, which was, and still is, full of abbreviations, shortcuts, inverted word orders, omissions of grammatical links, and so on. Other French crime writers among his contemporaries – for example, the Série Noire – employed slang and informal language much more. In *Maigret's Madwoman/La Folle de Maigret*, for example, a petty crook, whom Maigret disturbs having his breakfast, says to the police: "*Ne vous attendez pas, quant à vous, à ce que je vous offre quoi que ce soit.*" This is an extremely correct way of speaking, containing a subjunctive. In a way, this helps the translator, who can simply render it as "Don't expect me to offer you anything to eat", which is quite speakable without being marked as either over-formal or informal. Today, the character might say something like "No way are you getting any of this" – but that is too modern and US-influenced to be used for Simenon. The Maigret books do reflect one everyday aspect of police dialogue with suspects, which is to *tutoyer* them – i.e. call them the familiar "*tu*", not the polite "*vous*" – an indicator of treating them with, if not exactly contempt, at least condescension. In the series, which has a carefully worked out style sheet, we are discouraged from explaining *tutoiement*, although occasionally it is unavoidable. I did allow Maigret to call one criminal "Sunshine" when he finally managed to lay hands on him.

'Generally, I hope to keep the dialogue speakable and convincing, as coming from the character, but I also try quite hard not to allow idioms from today or even from the last 30 years to slip in. The English use of contractions (don't, won't, shouldn't, etc.) can be very helpful this way. I think all of us work like this – we don't introduce jarring modernisms.

'What is the appeal of a Maigret novel today? To start with, it is short – about 40,000 words maximum. And it usually opens with a very engaging, low-key scene (as do some of Hitchcock's films). Quite often, Maigret is simply sitting in his office on the Quai des Orfèvres in central Paris looking out at the Seine, perhaps on a bright June day (*Maigret's Revolver/ Le Revolver de Maigret*), a hot afternoon in August (*Maigret Sets a Trap/Maigret Tend un Piège*) or a damp foggy evening (*Maigret and the Saturday Caller/Maigret et le Client du Samedi*). Readers become familiar with the furniture, the other inspectors, the view over the city. In *Maigret's Pickpocket/Le Voleur de Maigret*, Maigret is jostled by a woman's shopping bag in the bus on the way home for lunch. And although there are period features (that bus has a platform, which — alas! — has disappeared from Paris buses today), Simenon is quite careful not to overdo them. One can easily imagine the action taking place any time in the mid- to late twentieth century. (In fact, more has probably changed for crime writers in the last 20 years or so, with mobile phones and the internet, than it did in mid-century when Simenon was writing.)

'The appeal is also — this has been said many times — Maigret's own attitude: characterised by patience (well, sometimes impatience!) and tolerance. He has his own share of human weaknesses — fewer than his creator, though, who once said Maigret was the opposite of himself. Drink and copious meals, for instance, feature regularly. In *Maigret's Revolver*, there is a pretty funny episode where he sits fuming for hours in the foyer of the Savoy Hotel in London waiting for a suspect to appear, trying to get a drink and falling foul of the incomprehensible English licensing laws.

'Nevertheless — or perhaps because of his own flaws (both Simenon's and Maigret's) — Maigret seeks to understand both criminal and victim. In *Maigret's Madwoman*, for example, he both regrets not taking seriously the worries of the old lady his colleagues think is mad, and at the same time is remarkably sympathetic to the unlikeable person who has, if not committed the crime, in a way provoked it. He may feel more hostility to certain perpetrators, but he always tries to discover how they reached the point of acting. He is interested in crime but not in punishment – reluctantly testifying in court and sometimes regretting the penalty (often death, during this period in France).

'Regarding the Maigret series, then, all 75 novels, I don't think it's hard to describe their appeal. But I must also put in a word for the so-called *romans durs* – standalone "hard" novels. Penguin has now translated several of these, and although I knew one or two of them before, translating them has been a revelation. In these books, there is not a detective story as such, although there is usually a violent incident or a death, and always a dark undertow. They often concern a man in midlife, reaching a crisis of some kind – all rather different. The darkness may come from inside, or from the surrounding society. The most recent one I translated, *The Little Man from Archangel/Le Petit Homme d'Arkhangelsk*, is about a Jewish bookseller in a provincial French town in the 1950s and several people have got in touch to say how struck they are by the creation, with very few brushstrokes, of the atmosphere of small-town France.

'So, if I were suggesting what to read to a new reader, I would recommend that they choose a couple of mid-period Maigret novels straight off (check the copyright page for the original date of publication) to get a feeling for the series. But also pick one of the *romans durs* – among the most famous is the hallucinatory *The Man Who Watched the Trains Go By/L'Homme qui Regardait Passer les Trains*. Less well known are *The Little Man from Archangel* or *The Mahé Circle/Le Cercle des Mahé*, set in a seaside town in the south of France. And quite extraordinary in its evocation of the port of Batumi in Georgia in early Soviet times, viewed through the eyes of the baffled Turkish consul, is *The People Opposite/Les Gens d'en Face*, of which the proofs are currently on my desk. It reminded me of Graham Greene.'

ADAPTING MAIGRET

I've known the talented crime writer Alison Joseph (of the entertaining Sister Agnes series) for some considerable time – and I have fond memories of meals with her by the River Isis at St Hilda's College in Oxford. These were judging lunches for the Crime Writers' Association Historical Dagger (I was a judge, she was an invigilator). Alison is also an accomplished adapter for radio who has appeared at Crime Scene at the National Film Theatre to talk about dramatising Maigret. I asked her to tell me about her assignment with Simenon for BBC Radio.

'It's a funny business, adaptation,' she told me. 'You take a story that has already been told, and tell it all over again. You remain fiercely loyal to the intentions of the author and yet at the same time you make ruthless changes where the new version requires them. It's a kind of mental contortion, a yoga of the mind. I was asked by BBC Radio Drama if I'd be interested in adapting some of the Maigret novels for radio. The plan was to do four, shared with fellow writer David Cregan, for broadcast late in 2002 to mark Simenon's centenary. Of course, I was delighted. Ned Chaillet was the producer, and he chose four stories that had never been done before, which, given the popularity of dramatisations of Maigret over the years, was a bit of a challenge. David did *A Man's Head/La Tête d'un Homme* and *My Friend Maigret/Mon Ami Maigret*, and

I did *The Two-Penny Bar/La Guinguette à Deux Sous* and *Madame Maigret's Friend/L'Amie de Madame Maigret.*

'There were various dilemmas that we had to discuss. One was that these four novels span many years within Simenon's career, which posed problems to do with time and place. We settled for a 1950s kind of feel, even though some were written earlier. We also had to decide on accents; we knew from the outset that Maigret shouldn't have a "faux" French accent, which meant that we were searching for equivalent English voices for Maigret, his wife, all the policemen he works with, and a cast of various villains and respectable folk. So Maigret, who was born in the country and finds himself in Paris early in his career, was given a rural burr; and the coppers in the police department were mostly urban London. The other immediate challenge was turning a novel into a 45-minute play. It meant the story had to be pared down, and there was very little breathing space. Simenon tells these stories with admirable economy, and I found that if I tried to cut part of the plot, it was like dropping a stitch: everything unravelled. I would have ended up with only half a story. It was Ned's idea to have Maigret in conversation with Simenon himself, debating each case. This gave us the chance to start the story further in, having set the scene in the prologue with Simenon, and also to return to Maigret and Simenon to "catch up" the narrative at various points where necessary. The reader who experiences a crime story in written form has the advantage of being able to revisit parts of the plot where it's not clear to them what's happened; the radio listener has no such privilege.

'If I may be allowed to use the word "postmodern" at this point, the dialogues between Maigret and his creator also opened up a possible seam for jokes, always important when you're dealing with villainy. Simenon wrote a book called *Maigret's Memoirs/Les Mémoires de Maigret*, in which Maigret at times takes issue with Simenon for his accounts of the various cases he covered. Maigret's main concern is that his life is, in fact, quite ordinary. He is, after all, only a policeman. He maintains that his cases mostly involve boring, repetitive footwork and observation – walking round Paris, keeping your eyes open. He claims that it's really nothing special, and that Simenon, by leaving out a lot of the everyday groundwork, makes it seem more glamorous than it really is. Simenon's view is that his embellishments of the story are only because he doesn't wish to bore the reader, which of course causes further offence to Maigret. In the radio plays, it allowed for moments of Maigret grumbling about how he was portrayed – the characteristic leather collar on a particular coat that had become his trademark, but which, as far as he knew, he'd only worn once, or all these pipes he was supposed to smoke... In the original *Memoirs*, we hear how Maigret met Louise, his wife, always referred to as Madame Maigret. In the *Memoirs*, Simenon gives a glowing account of Madame Maigret, to which Maigret, loyal husband that he is, takes no exception at all, apart from an instance where he points out that Simenon describes a bottle on their sideboard as sloe gin, when of course it's raspberry brandy, as anyone from Alsace would know. (Madame Maigret is very proud of her roots in Alsace.)

'Radio can only tell a story by what people say to each other, and so my first approach in dramatisation is to separate out whatever dialogue there is in the original. As soon as I started dissecting the Maigret stories, I realised that my task was going to be much harder than I thought. There is a deceptive simplicity to Simenon's style of storytelling, central to which is the way in which Maigret is the still silent heart of the story, rather than the agent of the action. Instead of the British rationality of Sherlock Holmes, Maigret seems to offer us a truth that is totally obscured, and yet which slowly, inexorably, emerges from the fog. Once I had pulled out the existing dialogue, to see how much of the story could be told by what Simenon allows his characters to say to each other, I realised that, mostly, what Maigret does is listen. And, even when someone does say something, so much is about what is not being said. So, at the beginning of working on the two radio plays, I was faced with the fact that an important part of the narrative was about silence. This was not a good start. The first novel I adapted was *The Two-Penny Bar*. The French word for bar in this case is *"guinguette"*, which, it turns out, has no English equivalent. It means a lean-to or shack where people drink. We settled for "bar". In this story, Maigret is on his own in Paris during the summer; his wife has already gone to Alsace for *les vacances* and is awaiting his arrival. He is endlessly delayed by the case, and she is endlessly forgiving. The case brings him into contact with a character called James, an urbane Englishman whose marriage is a sham. James is often to be found drinking Pernod on his own, and he and Maigret settle into a sort of amiable companionship through the weeks of the case. James expresses a great envy for Maigret, being able to live a free, bachelor life for the summer, in the absence of his wife. Maigret is unable to say so – another example of silence on the radio – but in fact the absence of his wife makes Paris seem empty and depressing. It is one of the many clever things about Simenon's writing: that the absence of Madame Maigret is a powerful presence in the story.

'In adapting *Madame Maigret's Friend* I was able to bring the marriage centre stage, and to look at how, out of the silences, Simenon paints a picture of a very close relationship. In this story, which concerns a Belgian bookbinder living in Paris who is accused of murder, one of the clues involves a particular hat that a woman was wearing. Madame Maigret decides that she had better help her husband, because hats are "women's work" and he'll never track it down by himself. Without telling him, she scours the milliners of Paris for an identical hat, with eventual success. Maigret comes home one evening to find that there is no dinner on the table; the first thing she says is to assert that he must be cross, while, of course, defying him to say anything of the sort. The rest of the dialogue in my version, in which she describes her quest, was very much faithful to the original, but what is allowed for in Simenon's prose is Maigret's silent gratitude and admiration for his wife. Radio doesn't do silent gratitude and admiration too well, so my work in this scene was all about conveying his feelings in words while allowing him still to be silent. I kept to the original, until the end. At the end of Simenon's version, they simply sit down to supper, with Maigret being silently grateful: which, of course, was no use to me.

'In my experience, people who share the intimacy of a long relationship always say one thing and mean something entirely different, and the Maigret marriage epitomises this.

'We had a lovely cast. Maigret was played by Nicholas Le Prevost, and Madame Maigret by Julie Legrand. Lucas, Maigret's inspector and right-hand man, was played by Ron

Cook. Georges Simenon was played by the novelist Julian Barnes.'

I asked Alison about a vexed subject: Simenon and women.

'I think you're right, Barry, in what you've said about some of the female characters Maigret encounters,' she replied. 'They are often women who have resorted to sex work, or who have rescued themselves from it. I think it's difficult for modern readers truly to realise how quietly revolutionary it is, to see Maigret simply encountering them as people – and also very interesting when one knows a bit about Georges Simenon's own particular behaviour where such women were concerned.

'There's a key moment in, I think, *Night at the Crossroads/ La Nuit du Carrefour* when a rather high-status woman starts to get changed in front of him. And he sees, by the way she rather carelessly takes off a few clothes, that she's so used to doing this in front of a man that she must have been a sex worker once. And what to me is *so* interesting is that Simenon, who writes so well about obsessive male behaviour, allows us to perceive that Maigret doesn't see this woman as an object of desire, but that he simply notices her behaviour and learns something from it. And yet we know from Simenon's own life that he was the opposite of this. It's a strangely Roman Catholic thing, I think, to create a character and to allow it to be his best self. It's a kind of paradox, a tinderbox spark that lights the whole *oeuvre*.

'I recently re-read *Maigret's Doubts/Les Scrupules de Maigret*, which seems to epitomise a lot of this very well. The novel has a compelling mood, of a damp, quiet January at police HQ, with the heating up too high and nothing happening at all. And then an odd, nervy chap arrives and tells Maigret that he is sure that his wife will, at some point soon, try to poison him. And so begins a classically Simenon tale, weaving a meditation on marriage with a palpable atmosphere of doubt and grumpiness, without even a murder to be investigated (yet). It shows how Simenon likes to play with ideas of evidence and rationality. In the sequences where Maigret, wondering whether his visitor is mad, tries to consult a learned text on psychiatric conditions. Simenon juxtaposes various academic definitions of mental illness with Maigret's heartland belief that none of this is as helpful as just sitting with the man and asking him a few questions.

'It goes back to the Catholicism of Simenon's storytelling, that he positions Maigret at the centre of a mystery that can only be solved by being still, in a mood of deep and troubled doubt, and waiting. It also has that quiet warmth, humour, and strong moral core that is typical of the Maigret tales.'

COLLECTING CRIME:
DESPERATELY SEEKING SIMENON

A writer to whom I have given a variety of commissions (mostly for *Crime Time*) is the prolific – and talented – Mike Ashley. I know I'm damned lucky to have got him to say yes so often! Mike has written and/or compiled many books covering a wide range of subjects, from science fiction and fantasy through mystery and horror to ancient history. He has a keen interest in the history and development of genre fiction, particularly in magazines, and has a collection of over 15,000 books and magazines. Among his mystery anthologies are *The Mammoth Book of Historical Whodunnits*, *The Mammoth Book of Historical Detectives*, *Shakespearean Detectives* and *Classical Whodunnits*.

To my surprise, Mike groaned when I mentioned Simenon.

'Let's forget about Maigret, Barry,' he said. 'Well, as much as we can. I returned with much trepidation to Georges Simenon. I say "returned" because, many years ago, when I was innocent enough to think all things were possible – at times I still think that, which says a lot for progress – I tried to work out a list of the most prolific writers of all time, complete with *accurate* statistics on the number of novels, short stories, essays, etc., etc., and even – yes – even wordage! I told you I was innocent. I found it near impossible to work out totals in detail for any prolific writer: from great pulpsters like Frederick Faust and H. Bedford-Jones to dime novelists like Prentiss Ingraham (who wrote an estimated 600 novels, all in longhand), to some of the more obvious candidates like Edgar Wallace, John Creasey, Robert Silverberg and, of course, Georges Simenon. Trudee Young in her bibliography *Georges Simenon* (Scarecrow Press, 1976) starts her introduction by saying, "Georges Simenon may well be the most prolific writer of the twentieth century." Notice that "may well be". It's a handy phrase tacked on to most of these prolific writers. But where are the facts? Young goes on to say – and remember, her bibliography was compiled 13 years before Simenon died – that he has written "over 200 novels and short stories, plus an additional 208 books written early in his career under pseudonyms". Combining novels and short stories isn't very helpful, but that possibly gives us something like 408 books, a figure deceptive in its apparent accuracy.

'Let's turn to Patrick Marnham, whose biography *The Man Who Wasn't Maigret* (Harvest, 1994) at least has the advantage of being written after Simenon's death. He says: "He had written 193 novels under his own name and over 200 under 18 pseudonyms." Over 200 what? Novels, stories? Is that the same as Young's "additional 208 books", I wonder. If so, then maybe we have some precision here: 193 under his own name, 208 under pseudonyms, so 401 altogether. Uhm, hang on. Martin Breese, in his indispensable *Breese's Guide to Modern First Editions*, breaks the figures down a little. He tells us that between 1924 and 1930 Simenon produced "190 novels and well over a thousand short stories all published under some 30 pseudonyms". Ah, it's 30 pseudonyms now. Clearly a whole barrel load of previously lost short stories had been broken open. Then he adds that, from 1930 to 1971, "he wrote 117 straight novels and two volumes of autobiography" plus 75 Maigret novels. In addition there were 143 non-Maigret short stories, including some pre-1930 but all under his own name, and 28 Maigret stories. So, let's see, that's 382 novels (190 + 117 + 75), plus 171 short stories under his own name and "over a thousand" under pseudonymous.

'Well, nothing ties in there. Those under his own name (117 + 75) total 192, not the 193 claimed earlier. Okay, one out – but come on, if you're seriously collecting Simenon that elusive "one" is the difference between madness and sanity. And Breese's computations start from 1924 and Simenon published his first novel and his earliest short stories in 1920. And how many feature Maigret? 75 novels and 28 stories? In *The Complete Maigret* (Boxtree, 1994), Peter Haining says 84 novels and 18 stories. Sometimes a book contains one Maigret novel and one non-Maigret. Back to 18 pseudonyms again: David Howard, in his article on Simenon in *Book and Magazine Collector* #228 (March 2003), quotes "193 novels under his own name and almost 200 under 24 pseudonyms".

'So, now we've had 18, 24 or 30 pseudonyms. Has anyone seen a definitive list? I haven't. The intrepid Pat Hawk in *Hawk's Authors' Pseudonyms for Book Collectors* lists 22. Ready? Aramis, Bobette, Christian Brulls, Georges Caraman, La Deshabilleuse, Germain d'Antibes, George d'Isly, Jacques Dersonnes, Luc Dorsan, Jean Dorsange, Jean du Perry, Georges Martin Georges, Gom Gut, Kim, Victor Kosta, Monsieur Le Coq, Plick et Plock, Poum et Zette, Jean Sandor, Georges Sim, G. Vialio and Gaston Vialis. Some of those were by-lines he used as a newspaper columnist, so they don't all relate to his fiction. But don't worry, I'm not about to try to add his reportage to this total output. But that may account for some of the confusion if not all of those names were used for fiction. But it's still only 22, not 24 or 30. I know of at least one missing from that list, J. K. Charles. No matter how we tabulate the figures, though, we still end up with around 400 novels, and countless (but over 1,000) short stories. It's a respectable total, but not in the super-league of mega-prolific writers. I mention all this not simply to confuse you with numbers – though I hope I have – but to show why I approach anything to do with Simenon with much caution. It's difficult to know what's real and what's fabrication. After all, we don't even know for sure on which day he was born. Family tradition suggests it was just after midnight on Friday, 13 February 1903, but his mother being so superstitious insisted that his birth be registered as just before midnight on the 12th. Is that true? Also, we can't be absolutely sure which was the first Maigret story to be written. They weren't published in the order he wrote them, not even in France, and he used the name of Maigret in earlier stories.

'Simenon often contradicted accounts of his activities over the years, and the more you read about him the less you feel you know, other than that he was a damned good self-publicist, regardless of the truth. The sex claims were headline grabbers that sound great – if not exhausting – and leave one wondering how he had any time left for writing. But then he was an exceedingly fast writer, and we have to believe that he was – even if, once again, I'm cautious over the statistics. In 1925, in another adroit piece of self-promotion, he secured a newspaper article that described his writing methods. Apparently he wrote 60 stories of 1,000 words each month, plus three stories of 20,000 words during the same month. That's 120,000 words a month or just over 1.4 million words a year. That certainly puts Simenon up among the top wordsmiths of the 1920s – he slowed down in later years to about a book a month. But hang on, if he was really producing 63 stories a month, that's 756 a year, and if he maintained that for even just five years in the 1920s, that's 3,780 stories and doesn't allow for all his novels. Hmm, once again I'm suspicious. Apparently, when he was at his most prolific he would scribble a story down and then, by way of revision, and to make it readable, he would read it back to a typist who produced the finished copy. But later, once he was travelling the seas, rivers and canals on his boat, he typed everything himself, which also slowed him down. Those early stories were very short, though, and he churned them out for various newspapers and magazines, including the pioneering French mystery magazine *Détective*, which began in 1929. You can get a feel for some of these in the translation by Peter Schulman of *Les Treize Coupables* (Fayard, 1932) as *The 13 Culprits* (Crippen & Landru, 2003). They feature the imposing examining magistrate Monsieur Froget, who, in each story, confronts the villain and, through his deft questioning, soon gets the criminal to make a mistake and then pounces on him (or her). There's no investigation – the whole case and evidence is presented skilfully in little more than 2,000 words, and, if you're quick, you'll spot the accidental slip of the tongue before Froget reveals it. There were two companion books, *Les Treize Enigmes* (1932) and *Les Treize Mystères* (1932), which have not been published in English so far as I know, although

Anthony Boucher did translate some of the stories for issues of *Ellery Queen's Mystery Magazine* in the 1940s. *Les Treize Enigmes* features Simenon's equally enigmatic detective, Inspector B. of the Sûreté, whose work is of such national security that he can only be referred to under the alias G7. *Les Treize Mystères* features the genuine armchair detective Joseph Leborgne, who has such a preternatural grasp of a case that he seems to solve it without having to think about it.

'Boucher's translations were the first appearances of *any* of Simenon's short stories in English, ever. The first of them, for the record, was 'The Case of Arnold Schuttringer' in the November 1942 *EQMM*. All too few of Simenon's short stories have made their way into English, aside from the Maigret ones. The collection *The Little Doctor* (first published in English by Hamish Hamilton in 1978) had appeared in France as *Le Petit Docteur* as far back as 1943. Two of them were translated for *The Strand* in 1947. These stories are longer and more complex, although, like the Maigret stories, they are solved by straightforward questioning and understanding. As with these stories, the Maigret novels have too easily pushed aside Simenon's other work, much of which was years ahead of his time. One has only to read *The Snow Was Dirty/La Neige Était Sale*, first published in 1948, to show how expert Simenon was at portraying a psychotic murderer. Or *Act of Passion/Lettre à Mon Juge* (1947), a deep psychological study of a murderer. Or *The Strangers in the House/Les Inconnus dans la Maison* (1940), a quite remarkable novel of family relationships and responsibility.

'Even if we don't know the exact numbers, Simenon wrote far more straight crime novels than the Maigret ones, and he should be better known for them and for his short fiction. But once you start collecting Simenon, be warned. You'll never know when it's complete.'

SIMENON: THE BOOKS

The Maigret Novels

As mentioned in the foreword, the following represents my posthumous collaboration with the late David Carter; the writing on the books below is sometimes mine, sometimes David's, and sometimes a synthesis of both of us. I've also included some aperçus by other writers who have made what struck me as pertinent judgements. For the actual titles of the books, I've mostly used the recent Penguin Classics editions, as they reflect an ongoing series that is available at the time of writing. The translators mentioned are also the impressive cadre currently being used by Penguin.

Pietr the Latvian/Pietr-le-Letton, 1931, translated by David Bellos (also translated as *The Strange Case of Peter the Lett*, *The Case of Peter the Lett* and *Maigret and the Enigmatic Lett*)

Plot: The police are expecting the arrival in Paris of the crook known as Pietr the Latvian. A body is discovered in a train at the Gare du Nord, which proves to be Pietr's double. The real Pietr has arrived but managed to escape police surveillance. Maigret tracks him down, but it soon becomes a very personal case, when one of his inspectors, Torrence, is killed while keeping watch on the Latvian. Then Maigret himself is wounded and a witness is killed. But Maigret soldiers on, more concerned to find the murderer than for his own health, and there is an unexpected twist at the end.

Comments: The plot is satisfyingly complex, and Simenon is at times more judgemental than in his later writings. Some of the characterisation verges on caricature, lacking the subtlety he was to develop subsequently. It is likely that this was the first fully fledged Maigret novel to be written; Simenon himself always claimed this. He finished the novel in the spring of 1930 and persuaded his publisher, Arthème Fayard, to publish it only on the condition that he would be able to publish several other Simenon titles at the same time. This is why a whole batch of Maigrets appeared in the same year. The novel is also remarkable for the fact that the author killed off one of Maigret's inspectors, Torrence, so early in the narrative (he was, of course, very quickly revived).

The Late Monsieur Gallet/M. Gallet, Décédé, 1931,
translated by Anthea Bell (also translated as *The Death of Monsieur Gallet* and *Maigret Stonewalled*)

Plot: The body of Émile Gallet is discovered in a hotel in Sancerre. Maigret is intrigued by the fact that he seems to have been leading a double life. It turns out that Gallet was not the sales representative that everyone took him to be, but a crook who had discovered ways in which he could blackmail certain wealthy individuals, and one rich lord in particular: Tiburce de Saint-Hilaire. Gallet himself, however, became a victim of blackmail and devised an insurance scam to benefit his own wife. The final truth that Maigret uncovers involves a remarkable twist.

Comments: The novel, which is one of the earliest Maigrets to be written, has vivid scenes set not only in Sancerre, but also in Paris and the Île-de-France. It is clearly based on Simenon's experience of meeting a group of French nationalists after his first arrival in Paris from Belgium. There are numerous striking twists in the plot, which are reminiscent of the conventions of the popular novels he had previously been writing.

The Hanged Man of Saint-Pholien/Le Pendu de Saint-Pholien, 1931, translated by Linda Coverdale (also translated as *The Crime of Inspector Maigret* and *Maigret and the Hundred Gibbets*)

Plot: Maigret gets involved, almost by chance, in investigating a murder that happened ten years previously. He becomes intrigued by the odd behaviour of someone he sees during a trip to Brussels: a rather shabby-looking man packs up some thousand-franc notes and posts them off as 'printed matter'. Maigret follows him to Bremen, Germany, and is present when he commits suicide. He discovers his identity and the fact that he had some connection with a rather suspicious group of individuals in Liège, who call themselves 'The Companions of the Apocalypse'. In Liège, Maigret learns that one of this group had killed another of the members during a nocturnal drinking session and then subsequently committed suicide. The man pursued by Maigret had started to blackmail his former comrades to gain revenge, and, when proof of his activities is uncovered by Maigret, he in turn decides to kill himself. The ending reveals Maigret at his most human and forgiving.

Comments: Some critics have found the plot a tad far-fetched, but in fact it is very closely based on events in Simenon's own life. The writer belonged to a similar group, called 'La Caque', when he lived in Liège. A member of the group died in mysterious circumstances: it looked like suicide but some thought that it was murder. The real young man's name was Kleine; in the novel, it is Klein. Whatever the truth of the matter, Simenon's fictional version involves a suspicious death. At the time there existed a law of 'prescription' in Belgium, which meant that a suspect could not be prosecuted for a crime after a lapse of ten years, and it is this fact that determines Maigret's action at the end of the novel. The real-life Kleine had died only nine years before publication of the book, however, which must have made Simenon unpopular with his old friends. The book is worth reading for its strong sense of atmosphere alone. It is notable, too, that the book deals not so much with the arrest of a single individual but with the complex, murky interactions of the members of a liégeois secret society.

The Carter of *La Providence*/Le Charretier de 'La Providence', 1931, translated by David Coward (also translated as *The Crime at Lock 14*, *Lock 14* and *Maigret Meets a Milord*)

Plot: A woman's body is discovered near a lock in the vicinity of Épernay. The husband of the victim, Sir Walter Lampson, who is the owner of a yacht, and his companions are under immediate suspicion. The occupants of a mysterious barge also seem to have some connection with the crime. A friend of Lampson, Willy Marco, is also murdered and the carter, Jean, has an accident. Maigret finds himself somewhat at a loss but finally manages to solve the mystery when he delves into the background of the carter.

Comments: *The Carter of* La Providence is a very accomplished novel in which Maigret clearly reveals his understanding of human suffering. It is also memorable for its evocation of dull, rainy weather along the canals and the atmosphere of towpath cafés. This early outing for Maigret suggests that he is more physically fit than he was to be in later novels, as evidenced by his repeated pedalling considerable distances along canal towpaths. The novel is particularly valuable as an evocation of France's past (not dissimilar to Thomas Hardy's similar endeavours in Britain), with the narrative construction geared more to these elements than to the crime-solving dénouement.

The Yellow Dog/Le Chien Jaune, translated by Linda Asher, 1931 (also translated as *A Face for a Clue*, *Maigret and the Concarneau Murders* and *Maigret and the Yellow Dog*)

Plot: Maigret goes to the old town of Concarneau to investigate the attempted murder of a prominent person. Just after his arrival, another regular visitor to the Admiral Hotel disappears in mysterious circumstances and a third is poisoned with strychnine. Maigret decides to put the surviving partner of the three men, Ernest Michoux, in jail, for his own safety.

While all this is happening, a mysterious dog with yellow fur is found roaming around the district. The local authorities become rather anxious at Maigret's apparent inaction. He, however, is intrigued by the behaviour of the waitress, Emma, at the hotel, who also seems to have a relationship with Léon, the owner of the yellow dog. Maigret finally discovers that at the heart of the mystery there is a drug-peddling racket.

Comments: *The Yellow Dog* is located outside the French capital, specifically in the Breton port of Concarneau, an area that Simenon was familiar with; what will strike the reader most is the evocation of life in a small provincial town, drawn with quiet skill. The crippling effects on a community of fear and malfeasance are handled with cool intelligence, while socio-economic conditions in Concarneau are described and the First World War impinges on the plot. As so often, the revelation involves the past, as well as the exploitation of an individual who appears to be anything but vulnerable. It is also a perfect example of a theme that is often found in Simenon's work: the illusion that Maigret is doing very little to move the case forward when, of course, there is a great deal going on beneath the surface. The novel also depicts the contrast between the methods of Maigret's assistant, Inspector Leroy, and those of the detective himself; this can be encapsulated as science versus psychological analysis. There is an interesting metatextual element here, too: at one point, Maigret uses the image of a violent storm in a film to evoke the events that are happening in the town. *The Yellow Dog* became one of the most well known of the early Maigrets due to the fact that it was filmed within a year of its first publication.

Night at the Crossroads/La Nuit du Carrefour, 1931, translated by Linda Coverdale (also translated as *The Crossroad Murders* and *Maigret at the Crossroads*)

Plot: A diamond dealer from Antwerp is found dead at the wheel of a car belonging to the insurance agent Michonnet at an isolated crossroads near Arpajon. Maigret discovers strange relationships linking the inhabitants of the three houses at the crossroads. There are the insurance agent and his wife; a Danish aristocrat, Carl Andersen, and his German wife Else, a former prostitute; and Oscar, a garage owner and former boxer. The mystery deepens when the wife of the diamond dealer is also killed and the aristocrat is seriously wounded. Maigret himself also narrowly escapes an attempt on his life. He manages to establish that the garage owner is involved in some shady dealings. The resolution sees justice done but love triumphant.

Comments: *Night at the Crossroads/La Nuit du Carrefour* is more conventionally written than most Simenon novels, and it utilises a savage violence that is not the norm for the author. Nevertheless, the plotting here has Simenon's typical assurance, with former prostitute Else the focus of the story. The unusual setting also adds to the book's fascination. *La Nuit du Carrefour* became very well known after Jean Renoir's 1932 film version.

A Crime in Holland/Un Crime en Hollande, 1931, translated by Siân Reynolds (also translated as *Maigret in Holland*)

Plot: Maigret is sent to the little Dutch village of Delfzijl to investigate the murder of Conrad Popinga, a lecturer at a local naval college, because a Frenchman, Jean Duclos, who was a guest of Popinga's, seems to be involved in the affair, in fact, it was he who discovered the murder weapon. But among the suspects are also the victim's mistress, a rejected lover, an old sailor, Popinga's wife, his sister-in-law, a lawyer, and a frightened cadet. Maigret gradually eliminates various false leads to arrive at the truth, but has a crisis of conscience when the murderer commits suicide.

Comments: This novel is not short of suspects and intriguing clues, including a sailor's hat in a bathtub and a cigar butt. The unravelling of the mystery is less interesting, however, than the evocation of the conservative nature of bourgeois life and values in a small Dutch town. Light and atmosphere are very well conveyed. It is also memorable for Maigret's own reflections on the responsibilities of the investigator.

The Grand Banks Café/Au Rendez-vous des Terre-Neuves, 1931, translated by David Coward (also translated as *The Sailors' Rendezvous* and *Maigret Answers a Plea*)

Plot: Captain Fallut is discovered strangled in a pool in the port of Fécamp. A young telegraph operator, who was prowling around his boat, is immediately under suspicion. Maigret is contacted by a friend of his, a local primary school teacher, and he sets out to prove the innocence of the young man, Pierre Le Clinche. He discovers that the captain was hiding his mistress, Adèle, on board the trawler, which roused the jealousy of both the telegraph operator and the chief engineer, who had discovered what the captain was up to. But a young ship's apprentice also discovered the captain's secret, and it was his threat to reveal all to the ship's crew that led to a series of tragic events culminating in Fallut's death.

Comments: 'It was indeed a photograph, a picture of a woman. But the face was completely hidden, scribbled all over in red ink. Someone had tried to obliterate the head, someone very angry. The pen had bitten into the paper. There were so many criss-crossed lines that not a single square millimetre had been left visible. On the other hand, below the head, the torso had not been touched. A pair of large breasts. A light-coloured silk dress, very tight and very low cut.' A dual achievement here: *The Grand Banks Café/Au Rendez-vous des Terre-Neuves* is notable for its maritime setting and its oppressively conjured atmosphere.

A Man's Head/La Tête d'un Homme, 1931, translated by David Coward (also translated as *A Battle of Nerves* and *Maigret's War of Nerves*)

Plot: Maigret does not believe that Joseph Heurtin, who has been condemned to death, is guilty of the double murder of Madame Henderson and her female companion. Maigret therefore enables Heurtin to escape and arranges to have him followed in the hope that this will help him discover the real guilty parties. He encounters the victim's nephew, Crosby, and a Czech student, and eventually uncovers a complex plan to put the blame on the unsuspecting Heurtin. The true criminal is finally caught and sentenced to death in Heurtin's place.

Comments: In a relatively unusual touch, a determined Maigret is allowed to correct a judicial error with the full support of the authorities. The novel incorporates a reference to a genuine murder case, an idea that was relatively unusual at the time. There is less attention than usual paid to subsidiary characters here, but the narrative exerts a grip and it's easy to forgive the coincidence on which the revelations rest. In a discussion between Maigret and the judge Coméliau, the detective inspector confides that, although he is obliged to draw logical conclusions from material evidence, as a human being he is more concerned with moral proof.

The Dancer at the Gai-Moulin/La Danseuse du Gai-Moulin, 1931, translated by Siân Reynolds (also translated as *At the Gai-Moulin* and *Maigret at the Gai-Moulin*)

Plot: Two young men, Delfosse and Chabot, deliberately allow themselves to be locked inside a nightclub called the 'Gai-Moulin' in Liège, with the intention of stealing the takings. In the darkness they stumble over a body and run off. The following day the body of one of the club's clientele, a Greek called Graphopoulos, is discovered in a public garden. The investigation culminates in the arrest of Delfosse and Chabot and one other man; the third suspect turns out to be none other than Maigret, who had been following the victim. He allows himself to be arrested by the Belgian police before revealing his true identity. The two young men are set free and Maigret investigates the role of Adèle, a dancer at the club, who seems to be involved in the affair and who leads him to the solution of the mystery.

Comments: In *The Dancer at the Gai-Moulin/La Danseuse du Gai-Moulin*, Maigret makes one of his most surprising and dramatic entries. The novel is also fascinating for its depiction of Simenon's home town, Liège, and for its study of one of the young men, Jean Chabot, who resembles in many ways the author himself at that age, as Simenon had also been tempted into crime at one time.

The Two-Penny Bar/La Guinguette à Deux Sous,

1932, translated by David Watson (also translated as *The Guinguette by the Seine*, *Maigret and the Tavern by the Seine*, *Maigret to the Rescue* and *The Bar on the Seine*)

Plot: On the eve of going to the guillotine, Jean Lenoir informs Maigret that he was witness to a crime six years previously. He and his partner had seen someone dumping a body into a canal. Lenoir subsequently blackmailed the murderer, who disappeared and was not seen again until one evening at a tavern by the Seine, the Guinguette à Deux Sous. Maigret goes to the tavern to investigate and mingles with local people and customers in this peaceful spot. He also meets up with a merry band of Parisians: James, Basso, and Mado and Marcel Feinstein. But their gaiety is short-lived when one of them is murdered. Maigret also manages to find Lenoir's accomplice, Victor Gaillard, and learns the name of the man who was killed six years before – a usurer called Ulrich. Maigret realises that he is in fact unravelling two crimes.

Comments: There may be some surprising (and unlikely) coincidences in the novel, but Simenon skilfully weaves together two interrelated plotlines and reveals yet again Maigret's unconventionally ambiguous attitude towards the criminal. There is one particularly strikingly realised character: English alcoholic James, who is able to conduct a relatively normal life despite his condition, and with whom Maigret shares the odd Pernod.

The Shadow Puppet/L'Ombre Chinoise, 1932, translated by Ros Schwartz (also translated as *The Shadow in the Courtyard* and *Maigret Mystified*)

Plot: Raymond Couchet has been murdered in his office in the Place des Vosges and a significant sum of money has been stolen. Maigret questions his first wife, Juliette Martin, their son Roger, and his mistress Nine Moinard, and he also keeps an eye on his widow. Roger commits suicide and this event leads to the revelation of what really happened, with the culprit unable to cope and descending into madness.

Comments: One of the attractions of *The Shadow Puppet/ L'Ombre Chinoise* is the adroit blending of three different locales: there are scenes in the world of petty officials, in the milieu of the higher levels of the bourgeoisie and in the area around Pigalle. Simenon lived in the Place des Vosges at one time and knew it well. The novel is acute in describing a variety of relationships among those living in an apartment building, including a woman whose aspirations to social climbing have unintended results.

The Saint-Fiacre Affair/L'Affaire Saint-Fiacre, 1932,
translated by Shaun Whiteside (also translated as *Maigret Goes Home*, *Maigret on Home Ground* and *Maigret and the Countess*)

Plot: The police at Moulins receive a message informing them that a crime will be committed in the church at Saint-Fiacre during the first mass on All Souls Day. When Maigret learns of this he decides to be there on the day. One reason for his interest is that Moulins is where he was born and he spent his childhood around the château, where his father was estate manager. Maigret attends the mass and watches the old countess, who, he suddenly realises, is dead. She has died from shock at seeing a false report in a newspaper announcing the death of her son Maurice. The investigation focuses on the immediate entourage of the countess: the son, who always seems to need money, Jean Métayer, the secretary and lover of the countess, and Gautier, the estate manager, and his son. The crime and its motive are finally uncovered during a dinner party organised by Maurice.

Comments: *The Saint-Fiacre Affair/L'Affaire Saint-Fiacre* features a nod to the classic British Golden Age crime novel, with all the various suspects assembled by the detective for a summation and the identification of the culprit. Also, the plot is resolved without the intervention of the law – Maigret is not officially working on the case. It is a minor Maigret novel, but as entertaining as ever, and it is celebrated among Maigret fans because of the biographical details revealed about the inspector's childhood.

The Flemish House/Chez les Flamands, 1932, translated by Shaun Whiteside (also translated as *Maigret and the Flemish Shop*)

Plot: The daughter of a night watchman in Givet has disappeared. The young woman, Germaine Piedboeuf, has had a child by Joseph Peeters. She never found acceptance among the group of Flemish people and there is a rumour that some rich shopkeepers arranged her disappearance. Maigret goes to Givet in a private capacity at the request of Anna Peeters. He gets to know Joseph, Anna's brother; Maria, his young sister, who is a primary school teacher; and his mother. It seems that the Peeters family played no part in the affair. Germaine's body is found in the river Meuse, with the skull smashed in, and a bargeman is suspected of the murder. When he finally solves the crime, Maigret decides to keep quiet about it, because he has not been officially appointed to investigate it. He allows the real perpetrator to leave for Paris, while the bargeman is still at large.

Comments: *The Flemish House/Chez les Flamands* is another example with Maigret behaving as Conan Doyle's Sherlock Holmes was occasionally wont to do: dispensing his own justice and not acting within the confines of the law. Although prefiguring anything that Simenon himself might have encountered, there is a pre-echo here of bitterness over linguistic issues in another country: much of the conflict in the novel comes from those who fight resolutely for the use of their own language and consider that it is being subsumed by what they see as a foreign tongue. There are also elements of class divide: the plot hinges on the notion that a wealthy family is being spared justice for crimes they have committed and on the resentment this creates.

The Madman of Bergerac/Le Fou de Bergerac, 1932, translated by Ros Schwartz

Plot: On his way to the Dordogne to take a holiday, Maigret sees a man jump out of a train as it slows down. He immediately follows him and is wounded. While recovering in hospital in Bergerac he learns that there have been several crimes committed locally by someone suspected of being a madman, and he realises that he himself may have been attacked by the man. There is general panic in the town, and Maigret helps the local authorities from the confines of his hospital bed. The corpse of a man called Meyer is found in a wood, and Maigret decides to concentrate his investigation on a group of local dignitaries. This reveals the true identity of Meyer and the person who killed him.

Comments: This is a novel in which Simenon utilises a device also adopted, in different eras, by Josephine Tey and Håkan Nesser. The notion of a detective conducting a 'long-distance' investigation by proxy is not a new one, but in the hands of a reliable practitioner it is still a fecund one – think also of Jeffery Deaver's Lincoln Rhyme. The fact that Maigret undertakes the entire investigation from a hospital bed seems to emphasise his genius for intuition.

The Misty Harbour/Le Port des Brumes, 1932,
translated by Linda Coverdale (also translated as *Death of a Harbour Master, Maigret and the Death of a Harbour Master* and *The Port of Shadows*)

Plot: Yves Joris, a former merchant sea captain, and now harbour master at the small port of Ouistreham on the English Channel, is found after he disappeared for seven weeks, but he has lost his memory. He has obviously been wounded and looked after. Maigret takes him back to Ouistreham, where he dies of strychnine poisoning just after his arrival. The inspector comes up against a wall of silence. Joris seems to have had some connection with Ernest Grandmaison, a rich shipowner and a former convict. Grandmaison's suicide prompts people to start talking. It seems that Joris had helped a criminal escape and had been wounded in the process. The person who wounded him feared being recognised by Joris and killed him.

Comments: A justly celebrated Simenon novel, with a memorable evocation of a foggy seaport. The fog becomes an understated metaphor for the cover-up of human motivations.

Liberty Bar/Liberty Bar, 1932, translated by David
Watson (also translated as *Maigret on the Riviera*)

Plot: An alcoholic Australian, William Brown, is stabbed to death in Antibes, on the French Riviera. Maigret attempts to reconstruct the events leading up to the crime, and meets Brown's mistress, Gina, and her mother, Jaja, who owns the

Liberty Bar. Here he also meets Sylvie, a young prostitute, and her pimp Joseph. He also encounters the victim's son, Harry, who is trying to track down a will. Not for the first time Maigret uncovers a double crime. Prison is the just desert in one case, but Maigret allows Brown's killer to go free. He has his reasons.

Comments: Making the most of its unusual setting on the Côte d'Azur, Simenon allows – not for the first time – Maigret's sense of pity to override his respect for the law. Although this is one of the author's favourite notions, it never comes across as simply a re-treading of a familiar theme; there is always something new each time it appears.

Lock No. 1/L'Écluse n° 1, 1933, translated by David Coward (also translated as *The Lock at Charenton* and *Maigret Sits It Out*)

Plot: Old Gassin falls off the gangway of his barge after a drunken evening. As he is trying to get out of the water, a man grabs hold of him. It is shipowner Émile Ducrau. When both men are finally fished out it is discovered that Ducrau has been stabbed and the police are alerted. Maigret concentrates especially on the background of Ducrau, and discovers that he is the father of Aline Gassin, a woman with mental health issues and the mother of a young boy. The tension mounts when Ducrau's son Jean commits suicide and an assistant lockkeeper is found hanged. The final confession brings with it a sense of release for the murderer.

Comments: The novel is deliberately disturbing in terms of its unflinching portrait of the nature of the relationships involved. The ominous, brooding feel of the piece is accentuated by the character of Ducrau, who ensures that his business is run in precisely the fashion that he dictates; both this fact and his uncompromising attitude render him unpopular in the community. He is disliked by both his bullied family and his servants, and it is hardly a surprise that there are those who wish him ill. The fact that such figures are something of a cliché in the crime fiction universe does not prevent Simenon from giving us a prime example.

Maigret/Maigret, 1934, translated by Ros Schwartz (also translated as *Maigret Returns*)

Plot: A certain Inspector Lauer, who is Maigret's nephew, is in a delicate professional situation. He was unable to prevent the murder of a man he had under surveillance, Pepito, the boss of a bar called the Floria. Furthermore, he is the prime suspect because of the way he panicked. While enjoying his retirement on the banks of the Loire, Maigret is visited by his nephew, who begs for his help. Maigret agrees, but encounters difficulties with his former colleagues. It proves to have been a gangland killing to silence Pepito.

Comments: This novel is unique in the Maigret series, with the former chief inspector solving a crime in his retirement. Simenon in fact intended it to be the last of the series; he wanted to devote himself entirely to the writing of *romans durs*. After 1933 he wrote no Maigret novels for five years, although he did write some short stories featuring the detective.

Cécile Is Dead/Cécile Est Morte, 1942, translated by Anthea Bell (also translated as *Maigret and the Spinster*)

Plot: For six months Maigret has been visited frequently by a 28-year-old spinster, Cécile Pardon, who lives with her aunt and is convinced that strangers have been regularly breaking into their house. No evidence is found to support her claims. But one day, when she is due to visit Maigret, she does not turn up. When Maigret goes to the house he finds that the two women have been strangled. During his investigations he brings to light the fact that the aunt was once the owner of a house of ill repute that was visited by some suspicious characters. One of these is a certain Charles Dandurand. It becomes clear that the same person did not murder both women.

Comments: Dissenting voices have observed that the novel's plot is confusing, but *Cécile Is Dead/Cécile Est Morte* also contains much of that haunting Parisian atmosphere that true Maigret aficionados relish. There is also a strong sense that Simenon is a novelist firmly in the realist tradition, with the setting here crucial to an understanding of the characters.

The Cellars of the Majestic/Les Caves du Majestic, 1942, translated by Howard Curtis (also translated as *Maigret and the Hotel Majestic* and *The Hotel Majestic*)

Plot: Maigret is asked to conduct a discreet investigation into the murder of an American woman, Mrs Clark, because she was the wife of an important American industrialist. She was found strangled in the staff changing room of the Hotel Majestic. Interest focuses first of all on a hotel employee, Prosper Donge, and his mistress Charlotte. But the next day there is another murder: that of the hotel porter. Against Maigret's advice, the examining magistrate has the couple arrested. Maigret then discovers that the American woman had formerly been Donge's mistress and that there is a child from that relationship. Someone had been blackmailing Mrs Clark, imitating Donge's handwriting, and her arrival in Paris threatened to unmask the criminal.

Comments: 'Try to imagine a guest, a wealthy woman, staying at the Majestic with her husband, her son, a nurse and a governess... In a suite that costs more than a thousand francs a day... At six in the morning, she's strangled, not in her room, but in the basement locker room.' The daily life of a grand hotel is very convincingly conveyed, especially from the quotidian perspective of those who work there. Maigret soaks up the atmosphere and discovers the murderer through his intuitive grasp of psychology.

The Judge's House/La Maison du Juge, 1942, translated by Howard Curtis (also translated as *Maigret in Exile*)

Plot: Maigret is a superintendent at Luçon and goes to solve a crime at the village of L'Aiguillon. A retired judge has discovered the body of an unknown man in his house. The judge has a son, Albert, and a daughter, Lise. He lives with his daughter, who has an intellectual disability and is taken advantage of by the young men in the village. One of these men, Marcel Airaud, disappears as soon as Maigret arrives. The judge eventually confesses to Maigret that 15 years before he murdered his wife's lover. The judge is arrested and Maigret discovers that the man found dead in the judge's house was a psychiatrist. The situation appears even more complex when it is revealed that Lise is pregnant. All these facts are woven neatly together in the conclusion, though in a rather complex way.

Comments: Difficult to follow at times, but if you love the crime fiction genre, this is a book that should be in your library – *The Judge's House* is an authentic Simenon classic. It is also evident here that the ethos of the book is very French; although Simenon occasionally adopted the accoutrements of the Golden Age of the British detective story, they were always seen through a Gallic prism.

Signed, Picpus/Signé Picpus, 1944, translated by David Coward (also translated as *To Any Lengths* and *Maigret and the Fortuneteller*)

Plot: A frightened bank clerk comes to Maigret with a piece of blotting paper, which he has found in a restaurant. On it the following words are written back to front: 'Tomorrow afternoon on the stroke of five I am going to kill the fortune-teller.' The police wait for possible bad news and wonder whether it is all a hoax. Confirmation arrives. When Maigret arrives on the scene he finds not only the dead fortune-teller but also a confused old man waiting patiently. He does not believe that the old man is the culprit, but Maigret does discover that the man changed his identity to help a widow get round the law. Then someone discovered what he was up to...

Comments: Simenon wrote this novel in 1941, and – rather like Charles Dickens – he serialised it in 34 instalments between December 1941 and January 1942. The following year, he opted to auction the manuscript, with proceeds going to benefit prisoners of war. The selling point here – and a particularly noteworthy element – is the edgy confrontation between Maigret and the examining magistrate, along with a curious and rather unique approach to the consciousness of its leading character, which Simenon permits us to enter.

Inspector Cadaver/L'Inspecteur Cadavre, 1944, translated by William Hobson (also translated as *Maigret's Rival*)

Plot: A man is run over by a train in a small town in the Vendée. A rich property owner, Monsieur Naud, whose father-in-law is a judge in Paris, asks Maigret to investigate the affair, because the rumour is spreading that he caused the man's death. Maigret encounters a private detective called Cavre, a former detective from his own department who is nicknamed 'Inspector Corpse' (because of the similarity between his real name and the French word for corpse, 'cadavre'). As ever, Maigret is not happy investigating the lives of people in high society. It turns out that the murdered man has seduced a young girl, who is pregnant by another man, and that there has been a general attempt to cover up the whole business. Maigret is sickened by the facts he uncovers and returns to Paris without making an arrest.

Comments: Another example of a favourite Simenon theme: Maigret passing judgement himself and thereby affecting the fate of the culprit. As Thomas Narcejac noted in *The Art of Simenon*, the writer was a 'connoisseur of souls', constantly showing a sense of compassion for those he writes about. Simenon admired and quoted the phrase: 'Understand and do not judge.'

Félicie/Félicie Est Là, 1944, translated by David Coward (also translated as *Maigret and the Toy Village*)

Plot: Maigret goes to investigate the murder of a retired accountant living on the Jeanneville estate, a few miles from Paris. He was shot in his own bedroom at point-blank range. It is a pretty ideal little world, which seems unreal to Maigret – like a toy village, in fact. He becomes fascinated by the character and behaviour of the old man's servant, Félicie, who is in love with the victim's nephew, Jacques. This young man is badly wounded in the Place Pigalle, but refuses to explain the circumstances. Félicie fears that he may be the murderer, but Maigret discovers that the events have more to do with the suspicious company he has been keeping. Jacques knows too much about someone's past criminal activities.

Comments: *Félicie/Félicie Est Là* is a charming and unusual novel with the main focus on the complex personality of the eponymous Félicie, who lies, contradicts herself, indulges in bizarre flights of the imagination and craves sympathy and understanding. The novel is a good starting point for those new to Simenon.

Maigret Gets Angry/Maigret Se Fâche, 1947,

translated by Ros Schwartz (also translated as *Maigret in Retirement*)

Plot: While in retirement, Maigret is asked by Bernadette Amorelle to investigate the suspicious circumstances surrounding the drowning of her granddaughter, Monita. He goes to Paris and along the Seine to investigate the girl's wealthy family background. He meets Bernadette's son-in-law, Ernest Malik, who turns out to have been to the same school as Maigret. Eventually he discovers that Monita was provoked into suicide by the revelation that she was in love with her own half-brother. This leads to a further death, from anger and a desire for revenge. All kinds of family secrets come to light, including adultery and an obsession with money.

Comments: Maigret finally manages to establish some kind of order in a family torn apart by passion and resentment, who have nevertheless struggled to maintain an appearance of respectability – a theme that recurs frequently in many of Simenon's *romans durs*.

Maigret in New York/Maigret à New York, 1947,

translated by Linda Coverdale (also translated as *Maigret in New York's Underworld* and *Inspector Maigret in New York's Underworld*)

Plot: While Maigret is enjoying his retirement on the banks of the Loire, he is contacted by a young man who is worried about his father, Joachim Maura, known as John, a New York businessman, who, from his letters, seems to be in some distress. Maigret agrees to go with the young man to New York to investigate. There, with the help of his friend Captain O'Brien of the FBI, he discovers some unsavoury facts about Joachim Maura's background. Some gangsters know these facts too and are blackmailing him. Maigret manages to get the gangsters arrested but he remains uneasy about his role in the whole affair.

Comments: Many aficionados are uncomfortable with Maigret venturing beyond his usual territory — and the detective himself doesn't seem to enjoy his trip very much. At the end, he is thinking more about the need to thin out his melon plants back home in Meung-sur-Loire. Much play is made with the very different approaches to enforcing the law in the two countries; the fact that Maigret has no authority in a foreign country is also a key element — Maigret demonstrates a certain impatience when lectured on the virtues of the American system. Caveats aside, it's a diverting outing.

Maigret's Holiday/Les Vacances de Maigret, 1947, translated by Ros Schwartz (also translated as *A Summer Holiday*, *No Vacation for Maigret* and *Maigret on Holiday*)

Plot: While Maigret and his wife are on holiday in Les Sables d'Olonne, Madame Maigret has to go into a convent nursing home for an operation on her appendix. While she is there a fellow patient, a certain Hélène Godreau, dies of a suspected skull fracture. Maigret's curiosity is aroused and he gets to know the brother-in-law of the victim, Dr Bellamy, who is known to be a jealous husband. The following night a young girl called Lucile is murdered and her brother Émile disappears mysteriously. It appears that the doctor's wife and Émile have been having an affair. Linking the crimes is a web of passions and jealousies.

Comments: Is this a too neatly tied-up mystery? It's still a cherishable entry, with Maigret conducting his investigations unofficially. The character of the doctor in the narrative is very well realised. The psychological undercurrents of crime are central to the narrative here, particularly as evidenced in the different responses Maigret obtains from the witnesses compared with those gathered in the official investigation.

Maigret's Dead Man/Maigret et Son Mort, 1948, translated by David Coward (also translated as *Maigret's Special Murder*)

Plot: An unknown man feels that his life is in danger and seeks the protection of the police, but Inspector Janvier cannot find him again. The following night the man is murdered. Maigret takes the case personally, regarding it as *his* murder. In the course of his investigations, he pursues a yellow Citroën, which leads him to the café in Charenton where the dead man, Albert, was the landlord. One suspect is chased by the police but is killed by his fellow crooks. Maigret, however, is able to identify the dead suspect and get on the trail of the so-called

'Picardy Killers'. Albert, it seems, knew more than was good for him.

Comments: Uncharacteristically, Maigret comes across in this novel very much as a man of action; it is an interesting change of pace, although some have criticised the evocations of Parisian locations as rather sketchy by Simenon's usual standards.

Maigret's First Case/La Première Enquête de Maigret, 1949, translated by Ros Schwartz

Plot: The story is set in 1913, when Maigret was still secretary to a superintendent in a small Paris police station. A young flautist informs the police that he has heard gunfire in a large townhouse, but when Maigret accompanies him there they can find no evidence of anything unusual having happened. The behaviour of the owners, a family called Gendreau-Balthazar, seems suspicious to Maigret, and he carries out a discreet investigation. He discovers that the Count d'Anseval was murdered because he refused to marry Lise Gendreau-Balthazar. There is a cover-up and an attempt to make the crime look like self-defence.

Comments: In this novel, we have a notable theme: it may be the first time in his career, but certainly not the last, that Maigret is disgusted at the behaviour of the French upper classes. This is not a typical Maigret investigation, but the future chief inspector is already revealing his talent for psychological intuition. The novel, which also provides insights into the life of the newly married Maigrets, ends with Maigret being appointed an inspector.

My Friend Maigret/Mon Ami Maigret, 1949, translated by Shaun Whiteside (also translated as *The Methods of Maigret*)

Plot: Maigret is being visited by Inspector Pyke of Scotland Yard, who has come over to study French methods of detection. His routine is disturbed by a telephone call from the Mediterranean island of Porquerolles, where an old tramp, Marcellin, has been murdered. The night before, he had been heard talking to people about his 'friend Maigret'. Maigret is glad to get away from Paris for a while, although the prospect of taking Inspector Pyke with him does not please him. They discover that a blackmail racket is behind the murder.

Comments: The backdrop of a small island with only a limited number of suspects may be a hoary cliché of crime fiction, but Simenon renders the seaside atmosphere, with its small square and café, irresistible. He is particularly acute at realising a locale where time seems to stand still and human action is stymied. Maigret is obviously ill at ease throughout in the presence of Inspector Pyke, but the juxtaposition of the two characters serves to highlight the differences in their methods: the plodding logic of the Englishman and the unconventional intuitive methods of the Frenchman. Might this be an example of détente?

Maigret at the Coroner's/Maigret Chez le Coroner, 1949, translated by Linda Coverdale (also translated as *Maigret and the Coroner*)

Plot: Maigret has been invited by the FBI to observe an investigation in the USA. A woman called Bessie has been murdered near Tucson, and five young airmen are being interrogated by the coroner. After interviewing several witnesses, it is discovered that the young woman had gone out with all five of the airmen and was mortally wounded while trying to resist the advances of one of them, who was determined to have his way with her.

Comments: Maigret is present only as an observer and even has to leave before the jury reaches its decision; many readers have therefore found the outcome rather disappointing. However, the novel, which has a sometimes dizzying complexity, provides interesting insights into the organisation of the American justice system. *Maigret at the Coroner's/Maigret Chez le Coroner* depicts the contrasts between a variety of aspects of life in the USA and France – something that Simenon explores elsewhere. This aspect adds an intriguing level of interest, not only for French and American readers.

Maigret and the Old Lady/Maigret et la Vieille Dame, 1950, translated by Ros Schwartz

Plot: Valentine Besson, an old lady, tells Maigret of her belief that the poison that killed her servant, Rose, was really intended for her. Suspicion falls on the old woman's children, but then another death occurs: Valentine kills Rose's brother, whom she apparently mistakes for a prowler. All is not quite what it seems in the old lady's family.

Comments: *Maigret and the Old Lady/Maigret et la Vieille Dame* has a rather contrived plot, but the character of the eponymous old lady is very convincing.

Madame Maigret's Friend/L'Amie de Madame Maigret, 1950, translated by Howard Curtis (also translated as *Madame Maigret's Own Case* and *The Friend of Madame Maigret*)

Plot: The police arrest a Belgian bookbinder called Steuvels following the appearance of some anonymous letters. They find blood and human remains in his house. But Steuvels denies everything, and the investigation makes no headway. When Maigret's wife comments on the strange behaviour of a young woman whom she often meets in a public garden, he is able to spot a link between two cases. The young woman is involved with a gang who killed a rich Italian widow, whose son-in-law is also an accomplice of the gang. It turns out that Steuvels also has links with the gang.

Comments: The connections between two cases in *Madame Maigret's Friend/L'Amie de Madame Maigret* are intriguingly developed, and the novel is memorable for the important role of Madame Maigret — Simenon was well aware of her importance.

Maigret's Memoirs/Les Mémoires de Maigret, 1950, translated by Howard Curtis

Plot: Having settled into retirement, Maigret decides to write his memoirs and compare his own memories with the portrait of him provided by a certain novelist called Georges Simenon. There is no plot as such, no mystery or its investigation: the reader is simply provided with reflections on various stages of Maigret's life, filling in a few gaps here and there in what can be learned from reading the novels. Maigret takes issue with some of Simenon's opinions and depictions of him and adds a few thoughts on the life of a policeman and the nature of justice. It is also a book about writing, about distinctions between art and reality: a fictional character talks about himself as though he were real, and the real author is introduced as a character in this fiction.

Comments: A charming book, utterly different from all the other Maigrets, but it should be pointed out that it will be of interest only to those who have read a large number of the Maigret novels before coming to it. Simenon's avoidance of the demands of the standard police procedural may not please all readers, but he introduces an element here that is frequently to be found in his work: an apparent randomness that finally translates into a kind of resolution. Critics of the novel have pointed out that an opportunity is missed here – what Maigret did during the years of the Nazi occupation is not discussed – but when one considers the more controversial aspects of his creator's past, it is perhaps not surprising that this issue is not addressed.

Maigret at Picratt's/Maigret au Picratt's, 1950, translated by William Hobson (also translated as *Maigret in Montmartre* and *Inspector Maigret and the Strangled Stripper*)

Plot: The action centres on a small nightclub called Picratt's in Montmartre. A striptease artist called Arlette informs the police that she has overheard two men planning to murder someone they refer to as 'the countess', and the name Oscar was mentioned. The police do not really believe there is anything in her story, but shortly afterwards she herself is found murdered. Working together again with the lugubrious Inspector Lognon, Maigret now takes Arlette's story seriously. Sure enough, it is not long before a countess is found murdered. And a crook called Oscar does seem to play an important role in the affair.

Comments: Most critics and fans agree in their high estimation of this novel, with its vibrant evocation of the iconic Parisian district of Montmartre. Simenon is not sentimental in his treatment of the area; he sees it as a place where human sympathy is sometimes in short supply and the exploitation of its residents is rife, something that those same residents simply accept as a fact of life. There is a particularly surprising element, given the writer's customary empathy with society's outcasts: the treatment of a character's homosexuality is notably unsympathetic. This is not necessarily unusual in novels of the period, but the indirect condemnation of a characteristic such as this is unusual for Simenon.

Maigret Takes a Room/Maigret en Meublé, 1951,

translated by Shaun Whiteside (also translated as *Maigret Rents a Room*)

Plot: After a robbery a young delinquent called Émile disappears. Then Inspector Janvier is badly wounded while watching the young man's lodgings in the Rue Lhomond. But it does not seem likely that a young man who had robbed a till with a toy pistol would shoot a policeman with a real gun. As Madame Maigret is away in Alsace visiting her sister who is due to have an operation, Maigret decides to take a room in the same building so that he can watch and question everybody. The young man is eventually found staying with his landlord. It turns out that someone misunderstood why Janvier was watching the house.

Comments: Simenon is a master at evoking the teeming life of Parisian lodging houses, and *Maigret Takes a Room/Maigret en Meublé* is a prime example of this skill. Maigret arrests the would-be murderer rather reluctantly after hearing the full story. An interesting touch is the fact that we are shown in some detail Maigret's attitudes to women other than his long-suffering wife; his courtesy and veiled flirtations perhaps do not correspond to interactions between the sexes in the twenty-first century, but, in providing a picture of a certain kind of honourable man in a different era, these elements make the book particularly valuable.

Maigret and the Tall Woman/Maigret et La Grande Perche, 1951, translated by David Watson (also translated as *Maigret and the Burglar's Wife* and *Inspector Maigret and the Burglar's Wife*)

Plot: A former prostitute, Ernestine, whom Maigret had arrested in the past comes to see him because she is worried about her husband. She goes by the nickname of La Grande

Perche (roughly equivalent to 'Beanpole'). Seventeen years before, when Maigret was an inexperienced policeman, she had removed all her clothes in an attempt to prevent him taking her to the police station. Now her husband, Alfred (known as 'Sad Freddie'), who is an unlucky burglar specialising in safecracking, has had a rather unfortunate experience while breaking into a house: he came across the blood-soaked body of a woman. He has therefore decided to go into hiding rather than get involved in a murder enquiry. According to Ernestine, the house belonged to a wealthy dentist living near the Bois de Boulogne. Maigret visits the dentist, Guillaume Serre, who has been living with his mother and his wife, who seems to have decided to leave him the very night of the attempted burglary. Finally, a whole string of murders is uncovered.

Comments: A particularly accomplished entry, with Maigret pitted against a very canny opponent. The treatment of Madame Maigret may not chime with contemporary attitudes, given that she puts up with all of her husband's absences and demands with nary a complaint, but she is always a fully drawn character. And the fact that the inspector takes his wife for granted is one of the character traits that prevents him from being too saintly a figure – which would be boring!

Maigret, Lognon and the Gangsters/Maigret, Lognon et les Gangsters, 1951, translated by William Hobson (also translated as *Inspector Maigret and the Killers* and *Maigret and the Gangsters*)

Plot: Inspector Lognon is as unlucky as ever. He still seems unable to advance his career. One night he witnesses an attack and perhaps a murder; this seems to be the chance he has been waiting for. He decides to act alone against some formidable American gangsters. But Maigret is called in and undertakes the investigation with the help of Lognon and the FBI. Two of the gang are caught and arrested and there is news of another murder, probably by the same gang, in the USA.

Comments: For once, Lognon decidedly proves his worth. Without his dogged persistence the police would not have known about the two murders that occur. Maigret is hurt and annoyed by the disrespectful attitude of the American police, which spurs him on to wind up the case successfully.

Maigret's Revolver/Le Revolver de Maigret, 1952, translated by Siân Reynolds

Plot: A young man wants to discuss something with Maigret at his home, but finding that he is not there, he manages to steal his revolver. Shortly afterwards, Maigret encounters a man called Lagrange who is worried about the disappearance of his son, and he realises that there is a link between the two incidents. It turns out that Lagrange is in fact a blackmailer who has also become a killer. Maigret manages to prevent a final tragedy, but it is difficult to prove the guilt of the person who is really behind it all.

Comments: One aspect of this novel that makes it unique for the anglophone reader is that part of the story takes place in London, where Maigret is helped by an old acquaintance, Inspector Pyke of Scotland Yard. In the course of his investigation, Maigret develops an almost fatherly affection for the young thief he is pursuing – a not uncommon response for the policeman. While a certain dry humour runs through many of the Maigret novels, it is more pronounced here, and the exhausted Maigret in a sweltering London is a nice touch, particularly as everyone around him tries to persuade him that the weather is uncharacteristically pleasant. Similarly, humour is found in Maigret having to smoke a cigar in the Savoy Grill as permission to use his pipe is withheld. Simenon incorporates a nicely French scepticism about restrictive British licensing laws (although a great deal of drink is consumed in the course of the novel).

Maigret and the Man on the Bench/Maigret et l'Homme du Banc, 1953, translated by David Watson (also translated as *Maigret and the Man on the Boulevard* and *The Man on the Boulevard*)

Plot: Louis Thouret is murdered in a cul-de-sac in Paris. There is no apparent motive for the crime. The man's wife proves to be contemptuous of her husband, and while she can readily identify the body, she admits to being puzzled by the fact that he was wearing light brown shoes and a garish tie she had never seen before. Maigret discovers that Thouret only pretended to go to work every day and had in fact been made redundant three years earlier. He had been surviving by committing burglaries.

Comments: *Maigret and the Man on the Bench/Maigret et l'Homme du Banc* provides a fascinating and thorough treatment of a common Simenon theme: the desperate attempt to escape from failure and a dull, uninteresting life. If the mechanics of the plot – involving an implausible money-making scheme – don't quite stand up to scrutiny, the same could just as easily be said of Sir Arthur Conan Doyle, whose plotting in his Sherlock Holmes stories sometimes strays from the credible.

Maigret Is Afraid/Maigret a Peur, 1953, translated by Ros Schwartz (also translated as *Maigret Afraid*)

Plot: Maigret is returning from an international police conference and decides to take a detour to visit an old friend, the magistrate Chabot, in the country town of Fontenay-le-Comte. His friend is mystified by a series of murders, which have all been committed using the same weapon but with victims who appear to have been chosen at random. One was an old aristocrat, another a midwife and one was an old drunkard. Although he is not officially involved, Maigret helps the local police, who are baffled by the case. Maigret is intrigued by the crimes, especially when he discovers that one of the victims was the brother-in-law of a certain Hubert Vernoux. He fears that there may be further murders, including his own.

Comments: Some have found this novel disappointing because Maigret remains somewhat aloof and distanced from the events, but there are many subtle Simenon characterisations to enjoy. In fact, Simenon makes the fact that Maigret is not officially working on the investigation a key plot point, along with the inspector's unwillingness to offer advice to the detectives on the case – although, inevitably, there are people (notably in the town involved) who come to appreciate his input. Once again, sympathy for the poor is an important theme.

Maigret's Mistake/Maigret Se Trompe, 1953, translated by Howard Curtis

Plot: A former prostitute, Louise Filon, is murdered in the sumptuous apartment that she has been living in for the past two years. There are no obvious clues at first so Maigret investigates the lives of her clients. Two men in particular interest him: her lover and the man who has been supporting her financially. Both of these are prime suspects because it is discovered that Louise was pregnant. The final resolution to the mystery is brought about by a confession.

Comments: In *Maigret's Mistake/Maigret Se Trompe*, the detective conducts an admirably rigorous investigation, and there is an intriguing contrast drawn in the social backgrounds of the two suspects.

Maigret Goes to School/Maigret à l'École, 1953, translated by Linda Coverdale

Plot: The novel takes place in the small village of Saint-André-sur-Mer, near La Rochelle. Gastin, the schoolteacher, is accused by the local police of killing the old postmistress, Léonie Birard, by shooting her. Everyone despised her because she was especially spiteful and malicious, taunting the children and slandering their parents. Gastin begs Maigret to prove his innocence by finding the real killer. Taking a sort of working holiday, Maigret moves into the small village. The victim lived quite close to the school, which was why Gastin is an obvious suspect, although he claims that he was not there at the time. Maigret solves the mystery by befriending one of the local children.

Comments: Maigret defies public opinion in the village of Saint-André-sur-Mer and follows his usual intuitive methods. The novel is memorable for the subtle relationship between Maigret and a local schoolboy, whom he interrogates with understated sensitivity.

Maigret and the Dead Girl/Maigret et la Jeune Morte, 1954, translated by Howard Curtis (also translated as *Maigret and the Young Girl* and *Inspector Maigret and the Dead Girl*)

Plot: A young girl is murdered in Inspector Lognon's sector, but as usual for the hapless inspector, Maigret takes over as it appears to be a complicated case. After conducting a very long investigation, Maigret discovers that the girl died following a series of unfortunate circumstances. She had received a letter informing her that she would inherit a large fortune from her father, a criminal who was dying. But the letter was intercepted.

Comments: As usual, Maigret's methods are shown to be very effective, unlike Inspector Lognon's plodding and routine approach. Maigret, in contrast, discovers the truth by attempting to understand the victim's personality. More than in most Maigret novels, the detective encounters a series of blind alleys as he attempts to learn about the background of the young murder victim. The slow accretion of facts here is handled with Simenon's customary authority.

Maigret and the Minister/Maigret Chez le Ministre, 1954, translated by Ros Schwartz (also translated as *Maigret and the Calamé Report*)

Plot: Maigret is asked by a minister to conduct a discreet enquiry to find a document, the Calamé Report, which has gone missing. The material would be political dynamite if it got into the wrong hands because it proves government responsibility for a major disaster. However, the press somehow learns of it, probably from the person who stole it, and the minister finds himself in an embarrassing situation. It appears that another unscrupulous politician is behind it all.

Comments: In *Maigret and the Minister/Maigret Chez le Ministre*, Maigret does not prove to be very successful, demonstrating his basic humanity (and fallibility), but the novel provides a devastating condemnation of the duplicity of political life – which seems as topical as ever.

Maigret and the Headless Corpse/Maigret et le Corps sans Tête, 1955, translated by Howard Curtis

Plot: Various parts of a man's body are fished out of the Canal Saint-Martin in Paris after they foul the propeller of a barge, but the head is missing. Maigret pursues his investigations in the area around a small bistro frequented by seamen and dockers on the Quai de Valmy. The owner of the bistro has gone missing. The headless corpse is finally identified by a scar. It proves to be the bistro owner, Omer Calas, and suspicion focuses on his wife and her lover, who had had a violent argument with Calas concerning an inheritance.

Comments: Simenon audaciously makes the crime in this novel almost incidental to his intriguing study of relationships, handled with characteristic authority. Maigret's preoccupation with a suspect goes beyond normal curiosity into something slightly unhealthy here – something that Madame Maigret remarks on.

Maigret Sets a Trap/Maigret Tend un Piège, 1955, translated by Siân Reynolds

Plot: Five women have been horribly murdered in the streets of Montmartre. Feeling angry and weary, Maigret decides to set a trap to try to catch the killer. A huge police operation is conducted but somehow the criminal manages to escape. However, a young policewoman in plain clothes who acts as bait manages to grab a button from her attacker's coat. A young man called Marcel Moncin is arrested, but then a sixth crime is committed.

Comments: *Maigret Sets a Trap* sees the inimitable inspector facing a seemingly unstoppable serial killer. The novel explores the author's central theme of the individual forced to act in extraordinary ways in the face of adversity.

Maigret's Failure/Un Échec de Maigret, 1956,
translated by William Hobson

Plot: An old acquaintance of Maigret's, an industrialist named Ferdinand Fumal, asks for protection after receiving anonymous letters. Despite the fact that Maigret has him watched, he is found dead the next day. In the course of his investigations, Maigret discovers that the man was detested by his staff and despised by his family. There appears to be an enormous number of suspects and the investigation makes slow progress, with Maigret unravelling the mystery rather belatedly.

Comments: Demonstrating that Simenon is perfectly prepared to be critical of his largely sympathetic hero, in *Maigret's Failure/ Un Échec de Maigret*, the detective's delay in solving the mystery is undoubtedly caused by his lack of concern about the victim, whom he disliked. While Simenon's criticisms of his hero are rarely overt, Maigret is never presented as a secular saint but as a man with faults and foibles – one of the reasons, in fact, why readers find him such a sympathetic figure.

Maigret Enjoys Himself/Maigret S'Amuse, 1957,
translated by David Watson (also translated as *Maigret's Little Joke* and *None of Maigret's Business*)

Plot: While taking a holiday on doctor's orders, but staying in Paris, Maigret is intrigued by an investigation being conducted by one of his inspectors, Janvier. It concerns the suspicious death of Evelyne, wife of a certain Dr Jave. She should have been on the Côte d'Azur and not in Paris at all. Maigret does not want to interfere directly in Janvier's case, so he sends him anonymous messages; these provide some help and eventually enable Janvier to discover how she was murdered and who did it.

Comments: In this intriguing outing, Maigret follows the case at a distance and gathers his information by reading newspapers, taking some desultory walks in Paris and making a few anonymous phone calls. He obviously enjoys conducting an investigation in this playful way, contrasting with his methods as detailed in other novels.

Maigret Travels/Maigret Voyage, 1958, translated by Howard Curtis (also translated as *Maigret and the Millionaires*)

Plot: Colonel Ward is found drowned in his bath in a luxury suite in the Hôtel George V, and his mistress, the Countess Palmieri, attempted suicide the previous night. Maigret makes enquiries about the countess's second husband, Joseph Van Meulen, a Belgian industrialist, and investigates the countess's shady past. The colonel's third wife also comes under suspicion.

Comments: Class is a recurrent theme in the Maigret novels, and in *Maigret Travels/Maigret Voyage*, Maigret – as is his wont – feels ill at ease in the world of high society, but he persists in employing his usual investigative methods.

Maigret's Doubts/Les Scrupules de Maigret, 1958, translated by Shaun Whiteside (also translated as *Maigret Has Scruples*)

Plot: Xavier Marton, a salesman of toy electric trains in a large store, believes that his wife Gisèle is planning to murder him because he has found zinc phosphide in the broom cupboard. After being contacted by Marton, Maigret is also approached by his wife. Maigret's investigation implicates two other people: Marton's sister-in-law Jenny and an acquaintance of Gisèle, who is also her lover. Soon Marton is found poisoned. It turns out, however, that a fatal error has occurred.

Comments: Many readers feel that *Maigret's Doubts/Les Scrupules de Maigret* concerns itself more with psychological investigation than with questions of justice, but this could be said of many of Simenon's works, and it is hardly a criticism. There is also a strange pre-echo of Philip K. Dick's novella 'The Minority Report', since Maigret finds himself investigating a crime that has not yet happened. There is also an unusual subplot involving the subtle ageing of both Maigret and his wife, with each beginning to suspect that the other is keeping a serious illness hidden from their partner.

Maigret and the Reluctant Witnesses/Maigret et les Témoins Récalcitrants, 1958, translated by William Hobson

Plot: An industrialist called Lachaume has been murdered in bed at his home in Ivry. The family owns a company making butter biscuits, and Lachaume was once a household name. The family lawyer is immediately called in and it is agreed to put up a wall of silence against all investigation. Maigret, however, will not be put off and eventually rules out the theory of burglary, believing that the culprit is to be found in Lachaume's immediate entourage. The focus narrows when it is discovered that the family business is on the verge of bankruptcy.

Comments: Maigret is not in a good mood during this case, for various reasons: his wife has just reminded him that he will be retiring in two years; his old office stove has been taken away; the new examining magistrate, Angelot, is breathing down his neck; and the Lachaumes are defensive and refuse to talk. It requires a great deal of his famed patience to discover the culprit. One of the most compelling Maigret outings.

Maigret's Secret/Une Confidence de Maigret,
1959, translated by David Watson (also translated as *Maigret Has Doubts*)

Plot: A manufacturer of pharmaceutical products, Adrien Josset, is suspected of having killed his wife Christine. The couple did not get on very well, and Josset had a mistress. Despite the evidence against him, Maigret is convinced that Josset is innocent; however, he cannot find the real murderer and only discovers who it is too late.

Comments: Confiding in his friend Dr Pardon proves to be a mistake on Maigret's part this time. There is an ideological stand here: the novel can be read as a firm statement against capital punishment. *Maigret's Secret* is an examination of the ways in which justice works – or, more pertinently, sometimes fails to work – and of how an innocent man can lose everything when the machinery of justice breaks down.

Maigret in Court/Maigret aux Assises, 1960, translated by Ros Schwartz

Plot: Maigret has to give an account in court of an investigation conducted several months previously, concerning the murder of Léontine Faverges and Cécile, the young girl who lived with her. Certain clues and an anonymous accusation seem to indicate that Léontine's nephew, Gaston Meurant, is responsible, but he is acquitted due to a lack of sufficient evidence. Maigret decides to pursue the investigation further and considers the role of Ginette, who married Meurant and has a background in the world of cabaret, and that of her present lover. The novel ends with a rather ironic twist.

Comments: Apart from the fascination of the story itself, the novel is provocative in its intelligent reflections on the processes of justice – and their limitations.

Maigret and the Old People/Maigret et les Vieillards, 1960, translated by Shaun Whiteside (also translated as *Maigret in Society*)

Plot: The old Count Armand de Saint-Hilaire is found dead, shot many times, in the study of his home near the Boulevard Saint-Germain. Maigret discovers that there had been a platonic relationship between the old count and Princess Isabelle, who has been recently widowed. They had planned to marry when she became free. In the meantime they had written to each other and observed each other occasionally from a distance. There seem to be no obvious suspects in the case, and the surly old housekeeper does not exactly help Maigret in his enquiries. When the truth finally comes to light, it is moving and sad.

Comments: Maigret feels considerable relief when this case is over. It is implied that the rarefied concept of love in this highly impressive novel seems almost unreal to him. In his collection of notes entitled *When I Was Old* (*Quand J'Étais Vieux*), Simenon wrote of this novel: 'I think it's the best of the Maigrets.'

Maigret and the Lazy Burglar/Maigret et le Voleur Paresseux, 1961, translated by Howard Curtis (also translated as *Maigret and the Idle Burglar*)

Plot: A burglar, Cuendet, is found dead in the Bois de Boulogne. The magistrates do not consider it an urgent case. Maigret, who is called in by another inspector, decides to focus on the victim's personality and discovers that the burglar had committed a final crime just before his death. For embarrassing personal reasons, a cover-up became necessary.

Comments: Even though Maigret eventually discovers the truth, he fails to convince the examining magistrate, despite the existence of material evidence. Throughout the whole novel there is a slight sense of despair in the confrontation between the police and the justice system.

Maigret and the Good People of Montparnasse/ Maigret et les Braves Gens, 1962, translated by Ros Schwartz (also translated as *Maigret and the Black Sheep*)

Plot: René Josselin, a quiet retired man, is killed in his home by two bullets. His son-in-law, who had spent part of the evening with him, had left him alone. Maigret begins to suspect that the murderer is someone close to the old man, and so he investigates the situations of the widow, Francine, and his younger brother, who has led a dissolute life and has frequently pressed René for money. Maigret eventually discovers the criminal, to whom a rather rough justice is meted out.

Comments: An unusual novel in the Simenon canon reveals Maigret adopting a slightly different approach: rather than focusing on the psychology of the murderer, the detective seeks to discover the weak spot in the life of a middle-class family, with Simenon providing a cool examination of the French bourgeoisie.

Maigret and the Saturday Caller/Maigret et le Client du Samedi, 1962, translated by Siân Reynolds

Plot: The owner of a small decorating business, Léonard Planchon, a nervous man with a hare lip, tries to call on Maigret on a Saturday, to no avail. He finally tracks him down at his home and reveals that he plans to murder both his wife, Renée, and her lover, the foreman of the business. Maigret promises to help, but one day later Planchon disappears, and Maigret feels that Renée and her lover must know something. Then Maigret discovers a document that appears to be forged, and which provides a motive for murder.

Comments: It is Maigret's sympathy for the victim that drives the investigation. As in so many cases, he comes up against the examining magistrate, who has little confidence in his methods. Not for the first time in Simenon's work, there is a sense that the Maigret novels could be described as anti-Agatha Christie, in that they avoid such tropes as the final dramatic revelation of the guilty party. With Maigret, the natural order – in which justice is re-established – is allowed to take its time.

Maigret and the Tramp/Maigret et le Clochard,
1963, translated by Howard Curtis (also translated as *Maigret and the Dosser* and *Maigret and the Bum*)

Plot: Some boatmen on the Seine pull a badly injured tramp from the water. Maigret tries to find the owners of a red car that was observed near the scene, but this does not yield any leads. Subsequently, it turns out that the tramp used to be a doctor, but he had decided to get away from it all. When the man recovers, he tells Maigret that he witnessed a murder, which is why someone tried to kill him. There is an ironic twist when the murder victim is finally discovered.

Comments: The loss of status is an unusual theme in Simenon, but in many ways one of the most interesting aspects of this novel is the treatment of the doctor who becomes a tramp. The book also provides an intriguing example of the theme of flight, which characterises many of Simenon's *romans durs*.

Maigret's Anger/La Colère de Maigret, 1963, translated by William Hobson (also translated as *Maigret Loses His Temper*)

Plot: The owner of a cabaret, Émile Boulay, is found strangled. He seems to have been leading a normal family life, but Maigret discovers that he had recently withdrawn a large sum of money from his bank account and that he had encountered some shady dealings. For this knowledge he was silenced.

Comments: Given the moral compass of his character, it is perhaps no surprise that the reason Maigret loses his temper is that someone associates his name directly with a case of corruption.

Maigret and the Ghost/Maigret et le Fantôme, 1964, translated by Ros Schwartz (also translated as *Maigret and the Apparition*)

Plot: Maigret wakes to the news that the hapless Inspector Lognon has just escaped an attempt on his life. He had been conducting surveillance of a couple, Norris Jonker, an art collector, and his wife Mireille. A young beautician has also disappeared. The only clue that Maigret has is a single word that Lognon was able to utter as he was brought out of the operating room: 'ghost'. Maigret eventually discovers that he is dealing with art forgers and attempted blackmail.

Comments: *Maigret and the Ghost/Maigret et le Fantôme* is not highly regarded by some connoisseurs, but the interest of a

Simenon novel is always in the detail, which is as keenly observed here as ever, even if this isn't vintage Simenon.

Maigret Defends Himself/Maigret Se Défend, 1964, translated by Howard Curtis (also translated as *Maigret on the Defensive*)

Plot: Maigret is awakened at night by a telephone call from Nicole Prieur, the daughter of a high government official. She is in a panic. After listening to her he settles her in a small hotel for the night. The next day he is summoned by the prefect of police because the young girl has accused him of attempting to seduce her. His job is on the line and he is suspended from duty. Maigret becomes suspicious of a dentist who knows the young woman and decides it is time he got his teeth checked! It turns out that his investigation of another crime is being given an inaccurate slant, and someone is trying to push him out.

Comments: Apart from being a rather unusual case, this novel also presents an intriguing portrait of a very intelligent murderer. Sexual abuse and accusations are a truly incendiary subject, with the appallingly low rate of rape convictions leading to such slogans as 'Believe Women', suggesting that accusations of harassment or assault should always be taken at face value, with the onus on the accused male to prove their innocence. Simenon, addressing the issue before it became so polarised, is able to offer a more balanced picture than might be acceptable today when a more Manichaean view of such issues holds sway.

Maigret's Patience/La Patience de Maigret, 1965,

translated by David Watson (also translated as *The Patience of Maigret* and *Maigret Bides His Time*)

Plot: An underworld contact of Maigret's, Manuel Palmari, is found murdered. He had been tracked by the police for about 20 years, but they never managed to convict him. Maigret himself knew Palmari to be behind a string of jewel robberies but was never able to catch him. In the course of his investigation, Maigret questions all the inhabitants of the apartment block and discovers some interesting links between them, but not in time to prevent another death.

Comments: *Maigret's Patience/La Patience de Maigret* is rightly considered a classic Maigret case, with rich and pointed descriptions of Paris.

Maigret and the Nahour Case/Maigret et l'Affaire Nahour, 1966, translated by William Hobson

Plot: Maigret is summoned in the middle of the night by his friend Dr Pardon, who has been looking after a woman who was lightly wounded by a gunshot as she was about to take a flight for Amsterdam. In the morning, a wealthy Lebanese gambler, Félix Nahour, is found murdered in a hotel room. Maigret discovers that the two cases are connected. The wounded woman, Lina, is Nahour's wife, and she was trying to run off with her young lover. Nahour's secretary, Fouad Ouéni, also seems to play a sinister role in the affair.

Comments: As with so many of the novels, the strength of this one lies in the psychological study of the murderer, one of the key attributes of Simenon as a writer.

Maigret's Pickpocket/Le Voleur de Maigret, 1967, translated by Siân Reynolds (also translated as *Maigret and the Pickpocket*)

Plot: While travelling on a bus, Maigret has his wallet stolen, but the following day the pickpocket contacts him. He proves to be a journalist and would-be screenplay writer who is suspected of the murder of his wife and who wants Maigret to prove his innocence. Maigret mingles in the world of filmmakers, discovering that the wife had been the lover of a film director. He follows several false trails but arrives finally at the simple truth.

Comments: Many feel that *Maigret's Pickpocket/Le Voleur de Maigret* is not one of the most accomplished entries in the series, but there is the customarily adroit characterisation to enjoy.

Maigret in Vichy/Maigret à Vichy, 1968, translated by Ros Schwartz (also translated as *Maigret Takes the Waters*)

Plot: While Maigret is taking the cure at Vichy, a middle-aged woman of independent means, Hélène Lange, is murdered. The local chief of police is an old acquaintance of Maigret and asks him to help solve the mystery. The woman's sister tells them that Hélène had a lover but hides some facts about their background. Maigret uncovers a case of deception that goes back many years.

Comments: The atmosphere of the spa town is charmingly conjured in *Maigret in Vichy/Maigret à Vichy*, and Madame Maigret proves to be very helpful in solving the case.

Maigret Hesitates/Maigret Hésite, 1968, translated by Howard Curtis

Plot: Maigret is warned by an anonymous letter that a crime is going to be committed. When he investigates the household of the lawyer Parendon, nothing appears to be out of order, except that the couple do not get on very well. But three days later the lawyer's secretary is found with her throat cut. Maigret reproaches himself for not being able to prevent the murder.

Comments: The memorable description of Paris in springtime is to be expected, but it's the account of an unhappy love that registers here with genuine poignancy. If, perhaps, the accusation might be made that things are wrapped up in rather cursory fashion, a particular virtue of the novel is the fact that in *Maigret Hesitates/Maigret Hésite*, the detective is not presented as an always wise and perceptive observer of human nature – he is more adrift than usual when finding himself in a different stratum of the class system. The novel, too, is notably sharp in its depiction of the functioning of a household, drawing more general aperçus about the ways in which families work than might normally be expected in a crime novel.

Maigret's Childhood Friend/L'Ami d'Enfance de Maigret, 1968, translated by Shaun Whiteside (also translated as *Maigret's Boyhood Friend*)

Plot: A former school friend of Maigret, Léon Florentin, seeks the detective's help: his mistress Josée has been murdered. Maigret discovers that she had four other gentleman friends who supported her financially, but that Florentin was her special lover. Although Florentin pretends to commit suicide and tells many lies, Maigret does not believe he is capable of murder. It seems, however, that he tried blackmailing one of Josée's gentlemen.

Comments: Maigret is hampered rather than helped by the presence of someone he knows from his schooldays – someone he had never really liked very much. Standard issue Maigret, but as skilfully written as ever.

Maigret and the Killer/Maigret et le Tueur, 1969, translated by Shaun Whiteside

Plot: A young student, who hangs around seedy bars and has a passion for recording the conversations he hears, is murdered. An anonymous caller claims responsibility. Maigret tries to make contact and to persuade the person to come forward, but he finds he has a pathological killer on his hands.

Comments: As so often with Simenon, the backbone of the novel is its disturbing, and multifaceted, depiction of a pathological mind.

Maigret and the Wine Merchant/Maigret et le Marchand de Vin, 1970, translated by Ros Schwartz

Plot: One of the richest wine merchants in Paris, Oscar Chabut, is found dead outside an elegant house used for discreet sexual rendezvous. Maigret discovers that the man's family is not particularly upset by their loss. The murder seems like an act of jealousy among rivals, but when Maigret investigates some of the reasons why Chabut was generally disliked, the identity of the killer becomes obvious.

Comments: The focus of the novel is on the psychology of humiliation, and how it can turn to anger and an act of revenge. Simenon handles the theme, of course, with assurance.

Maigret's Madwoman/La Folle de Maigret, 1970, translated by Siân Reynolds (also translated as Maigret and the Madwoman)

Plot: An old woman, Léontine Antoine, is not taken seriously by the police when she complains that someone seems to be persecuting her. She is continually finding household items shifted around. But then she is found dead. Maigret can find no obvious clues, although there is evidence of a firearm having been in the house. Attention is focused on the old lady's niece, Angèle, and her lover, who has connections with gangsters. A very unusual revolver is at the heart of the mystery.

Comments: Critics have long been divided about this novel: some find it lacks verisimilitude in its plotting, while the crime writer Edmund Crispin declared it 'one of the very best of the recent Maigret stories'. *Maigret's Madwoman/La Folle de Maigret* has, in fact, been notably lucky in its various translations, with the most recent by Siân Reynolds being one of the most nuanced and intelligent.

Maigret and the Loner/Maigret et l'Homme Tout Seul, 1971, translated by Howard Curtis

Plot: A tramp with well-manicured nails, Marcel Vivien, is killed in a derelict house in the Les Halles district of Paris. The man's wife proves hostile to Maigret's attempts to unravel the past of this former cabinetmaker. He discovers that the man had given up everything for the sake of a young girl called Nina, who then left him for a man called Mahossier. There then followed a chain of events that lasted over 20 years, resulting eventually in Vivien's death.

Comments: As is the case in many other novels, Simenon was clearly more interested in the life of a man who gave up his ordinary existence for an ideal than in the resolution of the murder mystery.

Maigret and the Informer/Maigret et l'Indicateur, 1971, translated by William Hobson (also translated as *Maigret and the Flea*)

Plot: A restaurant owner in Montmartre, Maurice Marcia, with gangland connections, is murdered. Maigret has had his suspicions about him for a long time but has not been able to prove anything. He finally gets a tip-off from an informer, who is eventually identified as a former pimp. The information proves to be reliable.

Comments: *Maigret and the Informer/Maigret et l'Indicateur* is noteworthy for the introduction of a new character among the inspectors: a certain Inspector Louis, widowed, dressed in black and melancholy, but who knows his district well. In some ways it could be said that Maigret does not really solve the mystery: if it had not been for the informer, he might never have made any headway, but fallibility in his protagonist is a frequent Simenon ploy.

Maigret and Monsieur Charles/Maigret et Monsieur Charles, 1972, translated by Ros Schwartz

Plot: Rather belatedly, Nathalie Sabin-Levesque asks Maigret to find her husband, who has been missing for over a month. Maigret investigates the family situation and discovers that husband and wife did not get on at all well. The husband, Gérard, spent much of his free time in bars and cabarets, where he was well known and liked as 'Monsieur Charles' ('a young man who would never grow old'). Meanwhile, his wife had become completely dependent on alcohol and was also deceiving her husband with a barman called Jo Fazio. Then Gérard's body is fished out of the Seine. Gradually, Maigret unravels a sad story of two ruined lives.

Comments: The revelation of the truth in the novel is brought about not by deduction or even by interrogation but by Maigret putting his psychological insight to practical use and exerting pressure on the suspect to act rashly (rather like Inspector Porfiry and the killer Raskolnikov in Dostoevsky's *Crime and Punishment*). This was to be not only the last of the Maigret series but also the final novel Simenon completed. After this, he devoted himself to dictating his memoirs. The book is a fitting and accomplished end to the Maigret series.

The Maigret Short Stories

The short stories featuring Maigret in earlier English editions have complex individual publication histories; the limited space here makes it unfeasible to trace them all. They were all originally published together in French, but without 'La Pipe de Maigret', in *Les Nouvelles Enquêtes de Maigret* in 1944. Most of them were written in 1936 and 1938. They did not appear together in English until their publication in the collection *Maigret's Pipe*, without the story 'Jeumont, 51 Minutes Wait!', in the Harcourt/Harvest editions in the 1970s. The stories, which include some of his most interesting, are: 'Death Penalty' ('Peine de Mort'); 'Mr Monday' ('Monsieur Lundi'); 'Jeumont, 51 Minutes Wait!' ('Jeumont, 51 Minutes d'Arrêt'); 'The Open Window' ('La Fenêtre Ouverte'); 'Madame Maigret's Admirer' ('L'Amoureux de Madame Maigret'); 'The Mysterious Affair in the Boulevard Beaumarchais' ('L'Affaire du Boulevard Beaumarchais'); 'Two Bodies on a Barge' ('La Péniche aux Deux Pendus'); 'Death of a Woodlander' ('Les Larmes de Bougie'); 'In the Rue Pigalle' ('Rue Pigalle'); 'Maigret's Mistake' ('Un Erreur de Maigret'); 'The Old Lady of Bayeux' ('La Vieille Dame de Bayeux');

'Stan the Killer' ('Stan le Tueur'); 'The Drowned Men's Inn' ('L'Auberge aux Noyés'); 'At the Étoile du Nord' ('L'Étoile du Nord'); 'Mademoiselle Berthe and her Lover' ('Mademoiselle Berthe et Son Amant'); 'The Three Daughters of the Lawyer' ('Le Notaire de Châteauneuf'); and 'Storm in the Channel' ('Tempête sur la Manche').

Death Threats and Other Stories, translated by Ros Schwartz

Comments: Just when Simenon aficionados were adding to their shelves the last couple of volumes of Penguin's very welcome new translations of all the Maigret novels, here comes a surprising and equally welcome codicil. *Death Threats and Other Stories* is a new selection of stories featuring Simenon's doughty French copper, and the key selling point here is that three of the stories are being published in English for the very first time. The subjects include an internecine conflict in a Parisian family, a possible murder in a hotel in Cannes and an explosive three-way relationship in a bucolic Loire setting. With translations by the ever reliable Ros Schwartz, this is a collection to be cherished, and I was glad to see my old literary editor from the *Independent*, Boyd Tonkin, adduced to sell the collection. 'Not just the world's bestselling detective series,' Boyd says, 'but an imperishable literary legend... Maigret exposes secrets and crime not by forensic wizardry, but by the melded powers of therapist, philosopher and confessor.' Trust Mr Tonkin to come up with such a penetrating aperçu for the appeal of Maigret. The volume includes: 'The Improbable Mr Owen' ('L'Improbable M. Owen', 1938), 'The Men at the

Grand Café' ('Ceux du Grand Café', 1938), 'The Man on the Streets' ('L'Homme dans la Rue', 1940), 'Candle Auction' ('Vente à la Bougie', 1941) and 'Death Threats' ('Menaces de Mort', 1942).

The New Investigations of Inspector Maigret, translated by Howard Curtis and Ros Schwartz

Comments: These new translations had not appeared at the time of writing, so I asked translator Howard Curtis for his comments: 'There were a whole bunch of Maigret short stories that first appeared in French periodicals from 1936 to 1939, some of which were collected in the 1944 volume *Les Nouvelles Enquêtes de Maigret*, two in *Maigret et les Petits Cochons sans Queue* in 1950, and the others uncollected. The translation by Ros Schwartz, which came out from Penguin in 2021 under the title *Death Threats*, contains three uncollected stories and the two from *Maigret et les Petits Cochons sans Queue*. Of the 17 stories in *Les Nouvelles Enquêtes de Maigret*, I've translated nine and I believe Ros Schwartz has translated the other eight. They are due to be published together by Penguin some time in 2022.'

Death of a Nobody/On Ne Tue Pas les Pauvres Types, 1947

Plot: A quiet and self-effacing man is killed in his own home. There seems no obvious reason for killing such a poor man, but Maigret discovers that he has been leading a double life.

Comments: The notion of leading a double life is a theme that recurs again and again in Simenon's works, and notably figures in the best of the *romans durs*.

Maigret's Pipe/La Pipe de Maigret, 1947

Plot: Madame Leroy seeks Maigret's help when she discovers that someone is searching her house when she is away. The following night her son Joseph disappears at the very same time as Maigret's pipe! Maigret discovers that Joseph has links with a crook who is looking for something in the house.

Comments: This pithy short story is not without humour. Needless to say, Maigret solves the crime… and gets back that celebrated pipe.

Maigret and the Surly Inspector/Maigret et l'Inspecteur Malchanceux, 1947 (also published as *Maigret et l'Inspecteur Malgracieux*)

Plot: A message comes through on a public emergency telephone. Someone shouts 'Merde to the cops!' and then there is a shot. A body is subsequently discovered near the Rue Caulaincourt. When Maigret arrives on the scene, he is handed the dead man's wallet, which reveals that the victim is a 38-year-old diamond broker. Inspector Lognon hopes the case might help him make a mark, but Maigret is always hovering in the background. When the mystery is unravelled as an insurance fraud, Maigret does his best to give Lognon the credit and invites him to dinner. But Lognon remains surly to the last.

Comments: The story is memorable for the introduction of Inspector Lognon, who also appears in six Maigret novels. He is nicknamed '*malchanceux*' (unlucky) because he never seems to get any good cases that would help him gain promotion. His colleagues also describe him as '*malgracieux*' (clumsy or ungainly) because of his dour and sombre manner. On its original publication in French, this short story was included together with three others: 'The Evidence of the Altar-Boy' ('Le Témoinage de l'Enfant de Choeur'); 'The Most Obstinate Customer in the World' ('Le Client le Plus Obstiné du Monde'); and 'Death of a Nobody' ('On Ne Tue Pas les Pauvres Gens'). Their English translations have complex individual publication histories, but they were first published together in English with five other Maigret stories in the volume entitled *Maigret's Christmas*.

A Maigret Christmas/Un Noël de Maigret, 1951, translated by David Coward (also translated as *Maigret's Christmas*)

Plot: A young girl, Colette Martin, living near the Maigrets, tells her neighbour that she saw Santa Claus in her room on Christmas Eve. Her Aunt Loraine follows the neighbour's suggestion and asks Maigret's advice. He discovers that the 'Santa Claus' in question was in fact a murderer with an ulterior motive. And Aunt Loraine proves not to be as innocent as she may look.

Comments: An intriguing little tale set in and around Maigret's apartment. The volume *Un Noël de Maigret* originally contained this story and two others.

The Romans Durs

The term 'roman dur', which was used by Simenon himself to refer to all those novels that he regarded as his specifically literary works, is difficult to render precisely in English. This is because its meaning in French is also not precise. Simply calling them Simenon's 'serious' novels is clearly inadequate, because it suggests that there must be something 'unserious' about the Maigret novels – which is demonstrably not the case. The word 'roman' translates easily enough as 'novel', but of the various possible meanings of 'dur' ('hard', 'tough', 'heavy', 'hard-going', 'harrowing', etc.), one term alone is not suitable to describe all the Simenon novels. What the author was probably trying to suggest is that these novels reflect disturbing aspects of life in a frank and unflinching way. As he was using a term that he had coined, it seems wisest to retain the French expression. There are precedents enough in the field of appreciation of the arts ('film noir', 'art nouveau', 'montage', etc.). So 'roman dur' it is.

As with the Maigret novels, I have used the recent Penguin translations where they exist and have included the names of Penguin's translators. For older translations, however, finding precise details is more tricky and translators have not always been credited in the past – and it should be noted again that older translators such as Sainsbury were not necessarily always faithful to the originals. In any case, I apologise in advance to any translators for not mentioning them in all instances. As well as the titles listed below, there are also several *romans durs* as yet untranslated into English.

The Man from Everywhere/Le Relais d'Alsace, 1931, translated by Stuart Gilbert

Plot: In a quiet Alsatian village a crime is committed for which a notorious international criminal known as 'The Commodore' is thought to be responsible. He was hoping to find anonymity in this out-of-the-way setting, but he cannot escape his former identity. Monsieur Labbé of the Paris Sûreté arrives, but he finds he is no real match for the master criminal.

Comments: This was in fact the first novel without the character of Maigret that was written under Simenon's real name. It is regarded by many as a classic, and a key demonstration of the author's considerable reach. It was two years after Maigret's initial appearance that Simenon wrote *The Man from Everywhere/Le Relais d'Alsace*, and his mastery of the vagaries of human psychology was already apparent.

The Mystery of the *Polarlys*/Le Passager du *Polarlys*, 1932

Plot: The story takes place on board a thousand-ton steamer, the *Polarlys*, which travels between Hamburg and Kirkenes in Norway. The voyage begins with the mysterious murder of a young Parisian woman, Marie Baron, and as the voyage progresses amid northern blizzards, the Norwegian captain feels that the evil eye is on his ship.

Comments: Although Maigret is not present, many have felt that *The Mystery of the* Polarlys/*Le Passager du* Polarlys has many of the rigorous characteristics of a Maigret novel.

The House by the Canal/La Maison du Canal, 1933

Plot: The story takes place in the small village of Neeroeteren in Belgium, near the border with Holland, in the province of Limburg. A young orphan girl goes to live with her cousins in the village. While one of the cousins is trying to embrace the girl he accidentally kills a young boy. Two other tragic incidents follow.

Comments: This novel has a distinctly personal feel, perhaps due to the fact that it takes place in Simenon's mother's birthplace, an element that clearly energised the writer. The inner life of the troubled heroine is sensitively handled, while the emotional brutality of other characters registers with genuine force.

Mr Hire's Engagement/Les Fiançailles de M. Hire, 1933, translated by Shaun Whiteside

Plot: A young woman has been found murdered in the Villejuif area of Paris, and the police soon suspect a man who lives alone not far from the scene of the crime This is Monsieur Hire, who has already been in prison on a vice charge and has made a living in various dubious ways. He spies on a young woman in the room opposite and gradually develops strong feelings for her. He also discovers that the real murderer is none other than the girl's boyfriend. He dreams of marrying her and escaping to Switzerland, but the novel ends tragically.

Comments: A brilliantly conceived and written novel, told from the perspective of its protagonist. The evocations of Parisian streets and bars are powerfully but economically realised through details of sounds, light and smells.

Tropic Moon/Le Coup de Lune, 1933, translated by Marc Romano/Stuart Gilbert

Plot: The novel takes place in Libreville, French Equatorial Africa (Gabon). A mild young man, Joseph Timar, who is new to the continent, gets involved with Adèle, who has a dubious past. She is a ruthless but good-hearted woman; she has, however, killed a young black man.

Comments: There is a critique in *Tropic Moon/Le Coup de Lune* of French colonialist rule folded into the standard plot – specifically of the state's willingness to twist the facts to defend itself. The issues are handled with intelligence and assurance but are not allowed to overwhelm the exigencies of the plotting.

The People Opposite/Les Gens d'en Face, 1933, translated by Siân Reynolds (also translated as *The Window Over the Way*)

Plot: Adil Bey has been assigned as Turkish Consul in Batumi, Georgia – part of the USSR. He finds himself in a sparsely furnished apartment and in a job made impossible by Soviet bureaucracy. No one will tell him how his predecessor died. Turkey's status in world affairs leaves him the subject of mockery from both locals and other ex-pats. He takes solace in his secretary Sonia, who lives with her sister and her husband (a member of the secret police) in the flat opposite his own.

Comments: This is a bleak psychological study humming with suspicion and disquiet, a searing account of the Soviet state, highlighting the fear, suspicion and alienation that ultimately allowed the USSR to control its people. *The People Opposite/Les Gens d'en Face* is an exceptional tale of betrayal set in Soviet Georgia. It is Simenon's most starkly political work – and the political context at the time of writing makes this an important read, this novel reminding the reader of some of the reasons why former Soviet countries want to fight for their independence. Simenon's background as a journalist undoubtably helps him set the scene of this novel with expert precision. He writes in the introduction that Adil Bey was partly inspired by a consul he met in northern Russia, and that the events were based to some extent on fact. As Simenon writes: 'I have written a novel. Batumi is a real place. The people are real. The story is real. Or rather, every detail is real, but the whole thing is invented. No, every detail is invented and the whole thing is real.'

The Night Club/L'Âne Rouge, 1933, translated by Jean Stewart

Plot: Set in Nantes, the novel focuses on life in a nightclub called 'L'Âne Rouge' (The Red Donkey). A young journalist, Jean Cholet, hangs around there among second-rate artists and gets to know a young woman called Lulu, who sings in the club. He drinks to forget his restrictive family life; he has a mother who is always complaining and a father whom he regards as a failure. But when his father suddenly dies, it provokes an unexpected crisis in his life.

Comments: This novel reveals various themes in Simenon's own life, with many aspects autobiographical. This is especially true of the character of the young journalist, who is fascinated by the seedy aspects of life and who has a weak mother and a father who dies unexpectedly. The story, however, is set in Nantes rather than Liège.

The Woman of the Grey House/Le Haut Mal, 1933

Plot: Germaine Pontreau has her heart set on owning the property that has just been inherited by her son-in-law, Jean Nalliers. She has decided to get rid of him; she regards him as just a nobody, and pushes him from a window on their farm. She then covers up the crime as an accident, which she is able to do convincingly because Jean suffered from epilepsy ('*le haut mal*' of the French title). Suspicions, however, are aroused.

Comments: This novel is part murder mystery and part a study in criminal psychology.

The Man from London/L'Homme de Londres, 1934,

translated by Howard Curtis (also translated as *Newhaven–Dieppe*)

Plot: Louis Maloin is signalman at Dieppe harbour station. From his signal box he can watch both the trawlers out at sea and the movements of people in the town. One evening he witnesses a murder take place directly below him on the quayside. He goes to investigate and manages to get hold of the suitcase that the murderer has stolen from his victim. It is full of money. From that moment on he is involved, and it will lead him to violence.

Comments: Admirers enthusiastically acknowledge *The Man from London/L'Homme de Londres* as classic Simenon, with its creative use of the port atmosphere and the Newhaven–Dieppe ferry, even if it is not quite as accomplished as such *romans durs* as *The Blue Room/La Chambre Bleue*. Crime was his métier, but Simenon was personally proud of his *romans durs*, which he considered to be more significant and more philosophical than the Maigret novels.

The Lodger/Le Locataire, 1934

Plot: A Turkish tobacco exporter, Élie Nagéar, is travelling to Brussels. During the voyage he becomes the lover of a young woman, Sylvie Baron, who has been working in a cabaret in Cairo. In Brussels his business does not do at all well and he kills a rich Dutchman and robs him. He then goes to join Sylvie and her mother at Charleroi. The mother finds out what Élie has done and cannot understand how a man like him could have resorted to murder.

Comments: As so often, the psychological study of the murderer is the main focus of this novel.

One Way Out/Les Suicidés, 1934

Plot: The novel recounts the story of a young bank clerk and his 17-year-old girlfriend, who cannot get married because of his poor financial situation. The girl's father is very hostile towards him, and this provokes him to set fire to the man's house. The couple flee to Paris, but more disasters follow, and they feel that the only true escape for them is suicide (as, indeed, the original French title made clear from the start).

Comments: One of the bleak, unsparing Simenon novels that truly merit the term *roman dur*.

The Pitards/Les Pitard, 1935, translated by David Bellos (also translated as *A Wife at Sea*)

Plot: The captain and owner of the freighter *Le Tonnerre de Dieu* (meaning, rather dramatically, 'God's Thunder') is setting out on his first voyage in the newly acquired vessel. Commander Lannec has bought it with money provided by his wife and mother-in-law. They are making their way from Rouen to Reykjavik. His wife Mathilde (whose maiden name is Pitard) has insisted on being on board, but she has a rather abrasive manner and in the narrow confines of the ship this soon leads to tension between them. The weather gets bad and Lannec cannot stand the way his wife treats him any more. To make things worse, his wife accuses him of just marrying her to get the Pitards' money. This all leads to a tragic conclusion.

Comments: Simenon here uses many of his own experiences of seafaring in these northern waters.

The Disintegration of J. P. G./L'Évadé, 1936, translated by Geoffrey Sainsbury

Plot: A German teacher in a school in La Rochelle suddenly starts behaving oddly and worries those around him. Just recently he has started to spend a lot of time in cafés with a young manicurist from a local hairdresser's. It turns out that Guillaume is an ex-convict who was arrested for murder and that the girl, Mado, is a prostitute who helped him to escape from Guiana. The teacher is completely distraught and fears discovery by the police. He also feels he could not cope with the family crisis that would ensue if the truth came out. He seeks to avoid the situation by fleeing to Paris.

Comments: It is something of a pity that *The Disintegration of J. P. G./L'Évadé* has not been more readily available, as it treats with rigour the theme of an extreme state of mind, which Simenon anatomised very successfully in some of his most acclaimed novels. The ethos of the crime novel – Simenon's other discipline – pervades the book to its advantage.

The Long Exile/Long Cours, 1936, translated by Eileen Ellenbogen

Plot: A young woman, Charlotte Godebieu, has killed her former lover and employer and decides to flee with a friend, Joseph Mittel, to South America. They get a passage on board a freighter used by smugglers. The long journey is difficult, especially for Joseph, who has been relegated to the boiler room. But Charlotte soon manages to improve her status by becoming the captain's mistress. Captain Mopps leaves them both to their fate in Colombia, where they have to survive among the indigenous population. To add to their concerns, Charlotte discovers she is pregnant. A change comes in their lives with the arrival of a letter from Captain Mopps, but it is not all to be for the good.

Comments: An involving – if unambitious – read, with a plot reminiscent of some of the popular novels that Simenon used to churn out before Maigret made him famous.

The Breton Sisters/Les Demoiselles de Concarneau, 1936, translated by Stuart Gilbert

Plot: A rich fisherman, Jules Guérec, driving home after enjoying himself in a nearby town, knocks down a little boy, who subsequently dies. He flees the scene of the accident and is too afraid to tell the police or admit it to his two sisters. Torn by guilt, he attempts to help the boy's family financially without telling the mother that he was responsible. Eventually, he even thinks of marrying the mother but comes up against the opposition of his two sisters, one of whom guesses the truth about what happened and tells the boy's mother. Guérec can no longer cope with the strain.

Comments: The novel deals intelligently with a theme to be found in several other Simenon novels: the results of attempting to avoid responsibility for a crime.

Aboard the Aquitaine/45° à l'Ombre, 1936, translated by Paul Auster and Lydia Davis

Plot: The novel takes place on board the liner *L'Aquitaine*, which plies between the Congo and Bordeaux. Dr Donadieu is the resident doctor on board and enjoys observing the lives of the passengers who make up a microcosm of colonial society. There is no real plot as such in this novel, which consists of a series of incidents, such as a child's illness, the behaviour of one of the officers, and an affair between a steward and a passenger.

Comments: The main interest of *Aboard the Aquitaine/45° à l'Ombre* lies in its depiction of the decline of French colonial society, seen from the point of view of the doctor. The novel is the final entry in the author's trio of African works (the other two are *Talatala* and *Tropic Moon*), and even for an author as economical as Simenon, it's clearly an exercise in focused concision. It is really no more than a novella, and its setting – entirely confined to the voyage of the steamer, making its way back to France from various colonial ports of call along Africa's west coast – suggests that Simenon wrote the whole thing in the space of a single similar voyage of his own. Also commendable is the avoidance of dramatic incident for its own sake; the low-key narrative here pays dividends for the reader prepared to concentrate and winkle out the book's hidden gems. Nothing much happens on the voyage, but this tale of a ship's doctor who can't help caring deeply about his transient patients manages to root about in more dark nooks and crannies of human nature than many works ten times its length.

The Shadow Falls/Le Testament Donadieu, 1937, translated by Stuart Gilbert

Plot: The novel plots the decline and break-up of a family after the death of the old ship owner, Oscar Donadieu (no relation to the doctor of the same name in the previous novel, *Aboard the Aquitaine*). His body is found in a pool in the port of La Rochelle, and murder is not ruled out. His four children and wife are surprised by the terms of his will: none of them will inherit anything until the last of them comes of age. So from then on the various family members fight for control of the family business. The family begins to disintegrate under a sequence of scandals, malpractices and attempts to settle scores. At the end, the youngest child, named after the old man but known to all as Kiki, and who has been in the background all along, returns. He has rejected everything that the family stands for.

Comments: This is one of Simenon's longest novels, and one of the few in which he endeavours to depict a whole range of characters with equal intensity. Characters who initially appear to be secondary come into their own eventually in the narrative. His sense of atmosphere and place never fails him, and if at times the behaviour of some members of the central family borders on farce, it is the absurdity of the 'human comedy' that is being depicted, which is why perhaps this novel, more than any other of his works, has often been compared to the work of Balzac – and there are also echoes of Flaubert.

The Murderer/L'Assassin, 1937

Plot: A 45-year-old doctor in the Dutch town of Sneek decides to murder his wife and her lover, a lawyer, and then commit suicide. He manages to kill the couple but not himself. He starts rumours that the couple have run off together and then quite openly conducts an affair with his servant, Neel. But when the bodies are discovered, suspicion naturally falls on him. There is, however, no real evidence against him. As time goes by, the servant takes the place of his wife and the local inhabitants avoid him. The doctor has to face the emptiness of his life.

Comments: *The Murderer/L'Assassin* is utterly compelling and represents Simenon at his most accomplished. The reader sees everything from the point of view of the murderer – a strategy that Simenon pulls off with some panache.

Talatala/Le Blanc à Lunettes, 1937, translated by Stuart Gilbert

Plot: A French coffee planter, Ferdinand Graux, nicknamed by the natives 'Talatala' ('the white man with the spectacles'), owns a plantation in the Belgian Congo. He has been leading a quiet solitary life until one day a private aeroplane is forced to make a landing nearby. The wife of an English diplomat, a certain Lady Makinson, is on board, and he falls in love with her, abandoning completely his fiancée back in France. The scene changes to Istanbul, but the novel ends back in the Congo again.

Comments: Unusually for Simenon, the novel deals with a clash between passion and reason, ending with an unpredictable resolution.

Home Town/Faubourg, 1937, translated by Stuart Gilbert

Plot: After an absence of 24 years, René de Ritter, who has had various dealings with the underworld, returns to his home town in the company of Léa, a prostitute. At first he does not reveal his identity, but he soon starts visiting members of his family and other acquaintances to try to squeeze money out of them. He even marries a woman he had known formerly, while the prostitute has an affair with a hotel owner. This casual lifestyle is doomed to end in tragedy.

Comments: With considerable aplomb, the novel blends straight narration with flashbacks in cinematic style. And – speaking of cinema – *Home Town/Faubourg* was a particular favourite of the French *Nouvelle Vague* director Claude Chabrol, whose dyspeptic world view and anatomisation of the French bourgeoisie echoed similar preoccupations on the part of the novelist. (Chabrol once remarked: 'My readings? I read all of Simenon, and when I'm done, I start all over again.')

Blind Path/Chemin sans Issue, 1938, translated by Stuart Gilbert

Plot: Two young white Russians have a close friendship dating back to the October Revolution. One day one of them is attracted to a woman, which leads to the break-up of their friendship.

Comments: The focus is on the friendship of the two protagonists. The final scene, in a night shelter in Warsaw, between Vladimir and the young man whom he has betrayed, is very impressively realised.

The Survivors/Les Rescapés du Télémaque, 1938, translated by Stuart Gilbert

Plot: Pierre and Charles Canut are the sons of a sailor who died in a shipwreck many years before. The last survivor of the incident is murdered, and it seems that Pierre, a popular local captain of a trawler, will be charged with committing the crime. Charles decides to try to discover the identity of the real murderer.

Comments: The style here is often reminiscent of a Maigret mystery, although the master investigator is conspicuously absent. There is a surrogate sleuth in the person of the sometimes successful, sometimes maladroit Charles, who finds himself investigating several suspects, including the dead man's alienated wife and more recent romantic entanglements. Charles is a nicely drawn character, and Simenon is as sure-footed as ever in his treatment of the uninspiring small-town milieu.

The Green Thermos/Le Suspect, 1938, translated by Stuart Gilbert

Plot: A moderate anarchist, Pierre Chave, tries to persuade a younger friend to give up his plan to blow up an aircraft factory at Courbevoie.

Comments: Terrorism is not a common theme in Simenon's writings, but he manages to brilliantly conjure the interaction of contemporary anarchist circles in Paris. There are pre-echoes here of the Swedish duo who virtually forged the Nordic noir literary movement in the Scandinavian countries, Maj Sjöwall and Per Wahlöö – specifically their novel *The Terrorists*.

Poisoned Relations/Les Sœurs Lacroix, 1938, translated by Geoffrey Sainsbury

Plot: Two sisters, Mathilde and Léopoldine (Poldine) Lacroix, live together in a house in Bayeux. One is married and the other is a widow, but they both love the same man, the husband of Mathilde. The atmosphere of the household is full of hatred and mistrust, and the children live in a constant state of fear. It does not come as a surprise to read that someone has discovered arsenic in the soup.

Comments: A harrowing story with scarcely a single likeable character, but which draws the reader on by a compulsive need to know what is going to happen.

Banana Tourist/Touriste de Bananes, 1938, translated by Stuart Gilbert

Plot: This novel is in fact a sequel to *The Shadow Falls*. Young Oscar Donadieu (known as Kiki in the first novel) is on his way to Tahiti, after rejecting all that his dead father stood for. He lives in a remote, abandoned hut on the island with a Tahitian prostitute, Tamatéa. He becomes revolted by the life of the colonial community in Tahiti, and gradually becomes disillusioned too with his own attempt to return to nature.

Comments: This is the only novel that Simenon ever wrote as a sequel (apart, perhaps, from some of the Maigret titles). One could argue that the title says it all: 'banana tourist' was the nickname the local people gave to those idealists who came to Tahiti in search of a simple life close to nature. The story only reinforces the pessimism of the original *The Shadow Falls*, and, as so often with Simenon, societal comments find their way into the narrative.

Monsieur La Souris/Monsieur La Souris, 1938 (also translated as *The Mouse*)

Plot: A tramp nicknamed 'Monsieur La Souris' (literally 'Mr Mouse') finds a sum of money near a corpse and hands it over to the police, without giving any further details of how he found it. He hopes that he will get the money back if it is not claimed.

Comments: The story is pure Maigret in spirit – in fact, it even features two of Maigret's inspectors, Lognon and Lucas. The outcome is unique among Simenon's works, the writer's move away from his signature character having the effect of energising his work.

Chit of a Girl/La Marie du Port, 1938, translated by Geoffrey Sainsbury (also translated as *Girl in Waiting*)

Plot: Marie Le Flem is the 17-year-old daughter of a fisherman who has just died in Port-en-Bessin. She gets a job as a waitress in a local café. She is generally bad-tempered, but shrewd and determined to get what she wants. Her older sister, Odile, is more good-natured and has a lover, Chatelard, who owns the café as well as a local cinema in Cherbourg. He believes he can easily win Marie's affections too, but she is coolly indifferent to him. He teases and taunts her, all to no avail. Complications ensue when Marcel, a new admirer of both girls, arrives on the scene.

Comments: The novel is attractive for the rich description of a fishing port, for which Simenon is so famous.

The Man Who Watched the Trains Go By/L'Homme qui Regardait Passer les Trains, 1938, translated by Siân Reynolds

Plot: *The Man Who Watched the Trains Go By* shows a man who is very much involved in society, a respectable family man, until the shipping firm where he is managing clerk collapses just before Christmas. A barrier falls in Popinga's mind and there emerges a calculating paranoiac, capable of random acts of violence, capable even of murder. As he feels himself drawn to Paris on Christmas Eve he enters into a disturbing game of cat and mouse with the law. Rushing towards his own extinction, he is determined to be recognised, for the world to appreciate his criminal genius.

Comments: Simenon's early thrillers show the sophistication and themes that made him famous. His characters are shrewdly accurate portraits of ordinary people and how they can be driven to extraordinary behaviour. Simenon's psychological portrayals of loneliness, guilt and innocence are at once acute and unsettling. Here, the psychological progression from a kind of normalcy to a bizarrely heightened consciousness in the unlucky protagonist is handled in the most authoritative of fashions.

The White Horse Inn/Le Cheval-Blanc, 1938

Plot: The Arbelet family stays at the White Horse Inn in Pouilly and discovers that an old night watchman is an uncle of Madame Arbelet.

Comments: Not vintage Simenon. The novel's main interest is found in its depiction of the local culture.

Three Crimes/Les Trois Crimes de Mes Amis, 1938, translated by David Carter

Plot: In 1922, impoverished art student Joseph Kleine is residing in the student quarter of Liège. When his corpse is found attached to the handle of a church door, it transpires that the night before he had been drinking with Georges Simenon. (The author was then working on the *Gazette de Liège* as a junior reporter, writing daily reports on incidents logged in local police stations.) What follows is as strange as anything in Simenon's actual fiction.

Comments: This was written in Paris in January 1937 and is included in this section as it is routinely categorised as a novel, but in reality it is a memoir, an autobiographical fragment in which Simenon even uses the real names of the people involved. The title *Three Crimes* is inaccurate: there were five crimes, murders committed by someone Simenon knew. Despite the interest here, Simenon had not yet mastered the autobiographical skills he was later to perfect, and the fragmentary nature of the book will not be to every taste.

The Krull House/Chez Krull, 1939, translated by Howard Curtis

Plot: A German cousin of the Krull family, Hans, arrives at the family home, which is above the family's grocery business. Hans seduces the young daughter of the family and is suspected by the community of having killed a girl whose corpse is found in the canal, but suspicion soon passes to his studious cousin Joseph.

Comments: A disturbing portrait of a family who are insecure because of their essential foreignness. Hans unsettles them all even more, and they clearly all want him to leave. The theme here of the scapegoat has broader cultural and social implications in this Simenon novel that is worth seeking out among the non-Maigret entries.

The Burgomaster of Furnes/Le Bourgmestre de Furnes, 1939, translated by Geoffrey Sainsbury

Plot: The burgomaster of Furnes, Joris Terlinck, is a strong, authoritarian figure. A young man, to whom he refused to give any money, commits suicide. The many ordeals he goes through do not soften or humanise him: his wife is very ill and dies; his daughter suffers from a mental illness and is finally sent to a mental hospital; and the local council is firmly opposed to him. But he does not yield.

Comments: *The Burgomaster of Furnes/Le Bourgmestre de Furnes* is a fascinating psychological study, not readily available for some considerable time.

The Family Lie/Malempin, 1940

Plot: Dr Malempin, who works in Paris, is preparing to leave on his holidays, but discovers that his son is suffering an attack of diphtheria. While watching over his son during his illness, the doctor recalls his own past and especially his relationship with his own father.

Comments: A warm and affectionate study, rare for Simenon.

The Strangers in the House/Les Inconnus dans la Maison, 1940, translated by Howard Curtis (also translated as *Stranger in the House*)

Plot: A former lawyer, Hector Loursat, has shut himself away from the world in a large house, where he spends his time getting drunk. One evening he hears a gunshot and finds a corpse in his attic. He learns from the examining magistrate that his daughter Nicole and her friend Émile Manu are somehow involved in the death of this stranger, who appears to be a criminal. When Émile is arrested, Loursat decides to take on his defence and makes a brilliant speech defending the younger generation and pointing out the parents' responsibility for their children.

Comments: A deservedly well-known novel, which deals with some important themes and includes a psychological study of alcoholism and the nature of parental responsibility. Of the non-Maigret books, *The Strangers in the House/Les Inconnus dans la Maison* is perhaps a work to be recommended to those unwilling to tackle Simenon's prodigious body of work in its entirety but who are seeking a representative novel.

Justice/Cour d'Assises, 1941, translated by Geoffrey Sainsbury

Plot: Petit Louis leads a life of petty crime. His speciality is conducting affairs with lonely, middle-aged women. He also gets involved in a gang's robbery of a post office. At the time of the story he is living with a mature wealthy woman and a young prostitute. But the girl's 'protector' comes out of prison, and Louis returns home to find the middle-aged woman murdered. In a panic he gets rid of the body, but the police are soon on his trail.

Comments: The processes of justice and the nature of guilt are adroitly handled central themes. A legal trial forms an important part of the novel.

The Country Doctor/Bergelon, 1941 (also translated as *The Delivery*)

Plot: Élie Bergelon is a local doctor of no particular talent. One day he accepts an offer made by a certain Dr Mandalin and passes some of his patients on to Mandalin. But a woman giving birth and her child die because Mandalin is drunk. The husband of the woman threatens to kill Bergelon, who then takes flight through France and Belgium.

Comments: The novel features the familiar Simenon themes of disappointment with life and attempts to escape from an unbearable reality.

The Outlaw/L'Outlaw, 1941, translated by Howard Curtis

Plot: Two refugees from Central Europe, Stan and Nouchi, are desperately looking for work in Paris. Stan hits upon the idea of tipping off the police about a Polish gang of criminals in order to get the reward, but it does not work. Despair finally drives Stan to murder.

Comments: Possibly dispiriting in its effect, this is the story of an individual's rather sad and hopeless plight. It does, however, demonstrate the author's clear sympathy for those who life has treated badly and whose futures are bleak.

Black Rain/Il Pleut Bergère..., 1941, translated by Geoffrey Sainsbury

Plot: Jérôme Lecoeur recalls his childhood in a small village in Normandy at the end of the nineteenth century, telling the story of his family and the search for an anarchist.

Comments: Told in the first person, some have found similarities between *Black Rain/Il Pleut Bergère...* and the autobiographical novel *Pedigree*, although the presentation of the protagonist's consciousness is subtly different.

Strange Inheritance/Le Voyageur de la Toussaint, 1941, translated by Geoffrey Sainsbury

Plot: The young Gilles Mauvoisin returns to La Rochelle on the eve of All Saints Day (*Toussaint*) after the recent accidental death of his parents. He inherits his uncle's business but is disgusted to discover all the scheming that has been going on in the family. He decides to escape abroad with Colette, the young widow of his uncle.

Comments: *Strange Inheritance/Le Voyageur de la Toussaint*, is close in theme, treatment and setting to *The Shadow Falls*. The central character, Gilles, is comparable to Kiki in that novel. The writer Graeme Macrae Burnet – who has told me of his love for Simenon's work – has an ambiguous attitude to this novel. He said: 'Any one of the multiple plot lines would more than suffice for an entire Simenon novel, yet they are all part of the tapestry of *Strange Inheritance*. The cast of characters, too, is larger than in most of Simenon's books, but bigger is not necessarily better. Which is not to say that *Strange Inheritance* is a bad book – it isn't – but while it is about 25 per cent longer than the average *roman dur*, the extra length still isn't sufficient to adequately explore the various narrative strands. It has the feel of a sprawling family saga, but not the stamina. It's as if Simenon wanted to break free of his single character study formula, but not of his punishing 11-day writing schedule. But there's still plenty of good stuff here.'

Ticket of Leave/La Veuve Couderc, 1942 (also translated as *The Widow*), translated by John Petrie

Plot: Jean has been released from prison after serving five years for murder. He gets a job as a farmhand with a widow called Madame Couderc, who is known as Tati. She lives together with her old father-in-law who lets her run the farm in return for sexual favours. Jean also becomes her lover but is soon attracted to a young girl living nearby, Félicie. Uncontrollable jealousy and violence erupt.

Comments: André Gide compared the novel to Camus' influential *L'Étranger*, as Jean is also a man who can never overcome his strangeness in the community. The book is indeed a stunning accomplishment, not least for its vivid descriptions of country life and atmosphere. One has the feeling that not a single word is superfluous.

Young Cardinaud/Le Fils Cardinaud, 1942, translated by Richard Brain

Plot: Hubert Cardinaud returns to his house one Sunday after church to find that his wife Marthe has left him, taking the housekeeping money with her, but leaving their two children in his care. Cardinaud sets out to find her, and discovers that she has gone off with a rather disreputable individual.

Comments: Yet another novel about flight, but this time from the point of view of the person left behind. A central theme is also the problem of human communication.

The Trial of Bébé Donge/La Vérité sur Bébé Donge, 1942 (also translated as *I Take This Woman*), translated by Geoffrey Sainsbury

Plot: Madame Donge, who is known by the nickname Bébé, tries to poison her husband, François, with arsenic while they are staying in their country house. But the husband recovers and she is arrested for attempted murder. The husband tries to understand his wife's behaviour and reflects on their life together. Meanwhile, Bébé is put on trial.

Comments: *The Trial of Bébé Donge/La Vérité sur Bébé Donge* is an unusual novel in that the crime leads to better understanding between the victim and his would-be murderer. Perhaps this aspect is one of the reasons why this novel was re-published in 1999 in France in a special edition designed for secondary school pupils, with extensive critical commentaries. Read Simenon to become a better human being?

Uncle Charles/Oncle Charles S'Est Enfermé, 1942, translated by Howard Curtis

Plot: Returning home, bookkeeper Charles Dupenn locks himself in his attic and ignores his wife and his grown-up daughters, who try to ascertain the reasons for his behaviour. His bullying brother-in-law Henri Dionnet, who runs a wholesale grocery business in Rouen, may offer a clue to Charles' behaviour.

Comments: Masterfully constructed (as so often with Simenon), this is a cogent demonstration of how few good deeds go unpunished in life. Characterisation is economical but drawn with great skill.

The Gendarme's Report/Le Rapport du Gendarme, 1944, translated by Geoffrey Sainsbury

Plot: A man is found badly wounded on a farm near Fontenay-le-Comte. He has also lost his memory. He knows he is there to seek out the Roy family, but does not know why. The local policeman gradually discovers some secrets about the family, which leads to acts of violence.

Comments: *The Gendarme's Report/Le Rapport du Gendarme* is a familiar, but satisfying, mixture of police investigation and psychological insight – a familiar combination in Simenon's work, but nearly always a sure-fire one.

Across the Street/La Fenêtre des Rouet, 1945, translated by John Petrie

Plot: An ageing spinster called Dominique has nothing better to do than spend her time watching what her neighbours are up to. One day she sees her neighbour Antoinette Rouet deliberately leave her husband in agony, when he is clearly suffering a heart attack. The young widow wastes no time in acquiring various lovers, and Dominique witnesses everything that is going on. But the whole affair makes Dominique acutely aware of the failure of her own life and leads to tragic consequences.

Comments: A sensitive study of a failed life – a theme that clearly attracted Simenon, who was always ready to examine the darker undercurrents of an individual's life, aware of what he perceived as such character failings beneath his own success.

Monsieur Monde Vanishes/La Fuite de Monsieur Monde, 1945, translated by Jean Stewart

Plot: On his forty-eighth birthday, Norbert Monde, head of a well-respected firm in Paris founded in 1843 by his grandfather, married twice, decides to give it all up and disappears with quite a large sum of money. He starts a new life in Marseille with a girl called Julie, who is a cabaret artiste. After he has his money stolen, Julie gets him a job in a rather shabby restaurant checking the orders. By chance he encounters his first wife, Thérèse, who is companion to a flamboyant middle-aged woman known as 'The Empress'. His wife has become a cocaine addict; Norbert decides to help her and also makes a decision about the future course of his own life.

Comments: In *Monsieur Monde Vanishes*, Simenon produces a study of bourgeois alienation, the story of a man who flees the stifling respectability of his life and enters a world of drug takers and dance-hall hostesses — where he can finally realise his ambition: to become an ordinary man in the street. The vision of the underworld on the Riviera conjured by Simenon here has few equals in French fiction.

The First-Born/L'Aîné des Ferchaux, 1945 (also translated as *Magnet of Doom*)

Plot: Dieudonné Ferchaux sets off in the company of his secretary, Michel Maudet, on a voyage from Paris to Panama. The old man is being sought by the police for the murder of three native people in the Congo some years earlier. The two men do not trust each other and decide to separate. But Maudet is planning to rob his boss, and violence ensues.

Comments: According to Simenon, this largely successful novel was inspired by a real event. Dealing with Simenon's conflicted protagonist Michel Maudet moving from resentment to murder, this is one of the writer's least compromising novels.

The Couple from Poitiers/Les Noces de Poitiers, 1946, translated by Eileen Ellenbogen

Plot: Twenty-year-old Gérard Auvinet marries Linette, who is already pregnant. They leave Poitiers and go to Paris, where they experience many disappointments. When Linette gives birth to a girl, Gérard has to take up a job in the provinces.

Comments: Some may find the initial sections of *The Couple from Poitiers/Les Noces de Poitiers* uninvolving, but Simenon inexorably exerts a grip in this tale of a couple facing a choice between risking tragedy and accepting a dull but safe existence.

Three Bedrooms in Manhattan/Trois Chambres à Manhattan, 1946, translated by Marc Romano and Lawrence G. Blochman (also translated as *Three Beds in Manhattan*)

Plot: An actor, François Combe, who was famous in France, has been living in New York for the past six months. He is trying to forget a scandal he was involved in. One day he meets a woman called Kay in a bar. She is a divorcee and also just hangs around in bars. They spend the night together and then find it difficult to separate.

Comments: Slight spoiler alert: *Three Bedrooms in Manhattan/ Trois Chambres à Manhattan* is one of the rare *romans durs* by Simenon that have an upbeat ending. It appears that the events are based closely on the meeting between Simenon and Denyse Ouimet.

The Mahé Circle/Le Cercle des Mahé, 1946, translated by Siân Reynolds

Plot: A French country doctor, brought up in a province peopled by his inescapable family, the Mahé circle of the title, goes on holiday to the south of France. A chance call on a sick woman there triggers an obsession. Haunted by a glimpse of her daughter, he struggles to survive between his conventional life, dominated by his remarkable mother, and the dazzling otherness of the south.

Comments: One of the previously untranslated *romans durs*, John Banville recently put this among his top five Simenon novels, calling it 'enigmatic, brooding and wholly convincing'. Translator Siân Reynolds said to me: 'My own view is that it can stand comparison with Camus's *L'Étranger*: the illness and death of the mother, told in agonisingly sober prose, lie at the centre of the novel.'

Act of Passion/Lettre à Mon Juge, 1947, translated by Louise Varèse

Plot: Charles Alavoine, a medical doctor, has killed his mistress, Martine, and writes a letter to his examining magistrate, whose duty is to collect testimonies and evidence but who does not prosecute or defend him in his trial. The novel consists entirely of this letter, in which Alavoine attempts to understand his own violent act. He reviews his life, from his childhood in the Vendée, through the experience of his father's death from alcoholism, being cared for by an overprotective mother, suffering the death of his first wife, and marrying the dominant Armande. He then makes the acquaintance of Martine, but becomes jealous of the eventful life she has led. How he comes to murder her is the crux of the whole novel.

Comments: *Act of Passion/Lettre à Mon Juge* is a major novel, written in the first person. Simenon manages not only to make the narration utterly convincing but also conjures up the presence of the other major characters with haunting precision, including the examining magistrate himself. Comparisons have been made with the writings of Albert Camus, and many critics regard it as Simenon's one indisputable masterpiece.

The Ostenders/Le Clan des Ostendais, 1947, translated by Geoffrey Sainsbury

Plot: Fleeing from the Germans in May 1940, a Flemish master fisherman sets off with his family and sailors on board five trawlers. They eventually seek refuge in La Rochelle, but when the occupying troops arrive, the local French inhabitants are not too happy with the situation. Then three of the boats are destroyed by mines.

Comments: An intriguing novel, valuable for what it reveals of Simenon's wartime experiences. He was officially in charge of organising accommodation for Belgian refugees in the very area where the novel is situated.

The Fate of the Malous/Le Destin des Malous, 1947

Plot: Eugène Malou, a property developer, commits suicide by shooting himself in the head. The shadow of this event hangs over the family for a long time. The youngest son, Alain, seeks to discover what his father was really like.

Comments: A moving, unsentimental story of Simenon's protagonist Alain's journey of discovery into fraught territory, during which he learns not only truths about his father but also about himself.

The Stowaway/Le Passager Clandestin, 1947

Plot: A certain Major Owen discovers a woman stowaway on board a cargo ship bound for Tahiti. They both have the same goal in mind: to find the heir of a wealthy movie mogul.

Comments: Simenon (with some relish) channels the exotic, implausible world of the popular novel, less rigorous than his own.

The Reckoning/Le Bilan Malétras, 1948

Plot: A wealthy retired retailer, Jules Malétras, has got married again, to Hermine de Dodeville. But he also keeps Lulu, a former servant, as his mistress. One evening when she refuses to yield to his desires, he strangles her without intending to. With the help of one of the young woman's friends, he gets rid of the body and decides not to give himself up to the police. Eventually, he comes to ponder over his whole life.

Comments: There is no intricate plot in this novel; the focus, rather, is on an assessment of a human life. The word '*bilan*' in the French title has associations with a balance sheet, and is therefore particularly apt for a review of a shopkeeper's life.

The Snow Was Dirty/La Neige Était Sale, 1948, translated by Howard Curtis (also translated as *The Snow Was Black*, *The Stain on the Snow* and *Dirty Snow*)

Plot: Frank Friedmaier lives with his mother, the manageress of a brothel, in an unnamed European town during the occupation in the Second World War. Just for the pleasure of it he stabs a non-commissioned officer to death and steals his revolver. Soon he commits another murder. He also wins the affections of Sissy, the daughter of his neighbour, but promptly passes her on to someone else. He is arrested by the occupying forces and undergoes a remarkable transformation.

Comments: *The Snow Was Dirty/La Neige* Était *Sale* is one of the most harrowing of Simenon's novels, focusing on a decidedly unsympathetic central character, but the narrative holds the reader's attention inexorably throughout. André Gide described it in a letter to Simenon as a 'remarkable' book.

Pedigree/Pedigree, 1948, translated by Robert Baldick

Plot: This is the most autobiographical of Simenon's novels, although the author himself did not like it described as such. It tells the story of the childhood in Liège of Roger Mamelin, from his birth in 1903, the same year as Simenon, to the end of the First World War. The novel evokes very vividly the experiences of growing up and all the sights and sounds of the city of Liège. Several characters can be recognised as portraits of the author's family. Many critics have felt that this work provides the key to understanding Simenon.

Comments: In his preface to the novel, Simenon stresses that it was written in a completely different fashion to his other works, and notes that it is completely unique in his output. He also explains how it was written at the encouragement of André Gide. Above all, while recognising that the central character has much in common with himself as a child, he still wanted it to be considered a novel: 'I would not even wish the label of autobiographical novel to be attached to it.' To make the distinction clear, he added: 'In my novel, everything is true while nothing is accurate.'

I asked my colleague Andy Lawrence (who I often commissioned in my days of editing *Nordic Noir* magazine) to talk about Simenon's *Pedigree*:

'Intended as the first volume of a trilogy, *Pedigree* stands apart from the rest of Simenon's output. Borne out of a long-standing ambition to write an extraordinary novel and a response to a personal crisis, the prolific author's magnum opus is a fictive redrafting of a memoir that has yet to be translated into English. After an accident chopping wood, Simenon experienced acute chest pains. Fearful that he might have broken a rib, he visited a radiologist in Fontenay-le-Comte. Misreading an X-ray, the radiologist told Simenon that because his heart was enlarged he would be dead within two years. For decades this misdiagnosis and the subsequent decision to write a memoir so that his son would know about his lineage was an accepted part of Simenon's mythology. Pierre Assouline's biography claims that the spectre of death was lifted two weeks later when Simenon consulted several doctors who advised that the initial prognosis may have been due to wrongly positioned photographic equipment. This reminder of mortality occurred during a period of renewed literary activity.

'After an abortive attempt to retire Inspector Maigret, Simenon sought to cement his literary reputation with a series of "*romans durs*". Determined to transcend the confines of genre fiction, the books written immediately after the publication of *Maigret* (*Maigret Returns*) were bleak studies of deviancy without the prospect of redemption. Declining sales for the *romans durs* forced Simenon to revive his most famous character. In the early days of the Second World War, as the conflict spread to Belgium, Luxembourg and the Netherlands, he completed work on *Cécile Is Dead/Cécile Est Morte* before being appointed "High Commissioner for Belgian Refugees for the Département of Charente-Inférieure".

Before the war, Simenon had mentioned in correspondence his ambition to write a different form of novel. Contractually committed to writing three Maigret novels, he had to wait until the manuscripts had been delivered before commencing work on what was intended as his signature work. The recent misdiagnosis and France's occupation may have preyed heavily on Simenon's mind as he sat down to create a historical account of his family. Dedicated to his son Marc, the finished text was eventually published as *Je Me Souviens*. It remains one of the few Simenon books not translated into English.

'After reading *Je Me Souviens* prior to publication, André Gide advised Simenon to abandon the book and redraft all material as fiction. The revised text was published in 1948 and is an essential read to understand the biographical significance of themes prevalent throughout the *romans durs* and Maigret novels. Chronicling a family in the Belgian city of Liège during the years 1903 to 1918, *Pedigree*'s length, time taken to write, subject matter and narrative structure mark it out as an atypical entry in the Simenon canon. Simenon typically wrote a novel in seven to ten days. The writing of *Pedigree* represented an exorcism, possibly a painful one. In a break from his ritualised routine it took him two years to finish the novel. A further five years would pass before it was published. Confronting his feelings about people and a city that he had left behind in 1922, Simenon may have intended to finally purge himself from the influence of a life that continuously manifested itself through his novels.

'In a repeat of the furore that greeted the publication of *Je Me Souviens*, Simenon was hit by several lawsuits from people who felt they had been libelled. *Pedigree*'s second edition removed offending passages and left blank spaces. The available version is *sans* the visibly noticeable blank spaces but has not restored the offending passages. Simultaneously *Bildungsroman* and a *roman-fleuve*, *Pedigree* largely corresponds with what is known about Simenon's early life. The chronology of certain events have been rearranged while others are purely fictitious. While some characters remain relatively unchanged from their real-life counterparts, others are composites or inventions. The absence of Simenon's brother has provided scope for analysis by numerous biographers. Representations of Christian Simenon appear in several Maigret novels, most notably *Pietr the Latvian/ Pietr-le-Letton*. His exclusion is either revisionism as wish-fulfilment, an acknowledgement of irreconcilable differences, or an attempt to avoid controversy concerning allegations that Christian collaborated with occupying forces during the war. Demonstrating that Liège's inhabitants, weather and topography would appear repeatedly in transposed form throughout the Maigret novels, *Pedigree* is also a portrait of influences and obsessions that remained with Simenon for the rest of his life.'

The Bottom of the Bottle/Le Fond de la Bouteille, 1949, translated by Cornelia Schaeffer

Plot: Set in Arizona, this novel tells of a respectable lawyer, Patrick Martin Ashbridge, who encounters his brother Donald, who has just escaped from prison. He takes him in and conceals his true identity from his family and friends, eventually helping him to escape across the border to Mexico. But the story ends tragically for the lawyer.

Comments: The fascination of the novel lies in the relationship of the two brothers who have lived utterly different lives. As so often elsewhere, Simenon demonstrates that the conflicted family remains particularly fertile territory for the drama of his fiction.

The Hatter's Ghosts/Les Fantômes du Chapelier, 1949, translated by Howard Curtis (also translated as *The Hatter's Phantoms*)

Plot: An apparently respectable hat-maker in La Rochelle, Léon Labbé, is gradually revealed to be a serial murderer, having killed six women. Initially, there is no apparent link between the killings, although one becomes obvious as the novel progresses. Labbé's neighbour, the tailor Kachoudas, becomes convinced that the hatter is indeed the murderer, and he stalks his neighbour, not daring to take any action. Labbé writes confident and taunting letters to the local newspaper. He wants people to understand that the murders are necessary; indeed, the reader discovers that there is a twisted logic to them. But the hatter begins to lose control of his well-ordered world and becomes paranoid – the ghosts are really other people as he sees them.

Comments: A concise but utterly assured novel, notably difficult to put down. Although it is written in the third person, everything is told from the point of view of the eponymous hatter. One finishes the novel with the feeling of having experienced directly the mind of a deranged man rather than just reading about him. The detail of the backstreets and cafés of La Rochelle is also hauntingly realised. Howard Curtis's new translation is due in 2022.

Four Days in a Lifetime/Les Quatre Jours du Pauvre Homme, 1949, translated by Louise Varèse

Plot: This novel tells the story, in two parts, of the general decline of François Lecoin, from being unemployed to getting involved in a blackmailing racket.

Comments: A truly misanthropic novel with no gleam of hope, describing with rigour a failed life that ends in tragedy. Despite this, the experience of reading *Four Days in a Lifetime/Les Quatre Jours du Pauvre Homme* is not a downbeat one.

The Burial of Monsieur Bouvet/L'Enterrement de Monsieur Bouvet, 1950, translated by Eugene MacCown (also translated as *Inquest on Bouvet*)

Plot: An elderly man suddenly falls down dead on the banks of the Seine, witnessed by many people. And one man takes a photograph. It seems that the man has no family, but the photograph appears in the press and his wife and daughter appear on the scene. It turns out that he had lived under various different identities and had led a very eventful life. The burial is delayed until as much can be discovered about him as possible.

Comments: *The Burial of Monsieur Bouvet/L'Enterrement de Monsieur Bouvet* represents Simenon at his most subtle and perceptive. It is a moving story of selfish interest and simple human love. The final sequence is especially well written, with telling circumstantial detail. Although not a Maigret novel, the investigation into the old man's identity is largely conducted by one of the detective's right-hand men, Lucas. The novel is particularly effective in its steady revelation of incident, and points are made about the nebulous nature of identity via the eponymous Bouvet's reinvention of his life.

The Heart of a Man/Les Volets Verts, 1950, translated by Louise Varèse

Plot: Émile Maugin is a famous actor of both stage and screen and has lived life to the full, not only working hard but also drinking and having countless lovers. He is cynical and appears distant to many, but after a strong warning from his heart specialist, he reviews his life and finds he feels an intense sense of guilt that he cannot fathom. He continues to make the most of his time, but questions himself and wonders when the moment of death will come.

Comments: An astringent and powerful novel, with many insights into ways in which actors create characters. There are many parallels with the psychology of the writer. It also has something distinctively Kafkaesque in the imaginary 'trial' sequences, and especially in the final stages of the actor's life. It is a pity that the English translation of the original title distracts attention from the mysterious symbolism of the 'green shutters', which haunt the novel and are central to an understanding of it.

Aunt Jeanne/Tante Jeanne, 1951, translated by Geoffrey Sainsbury

Plot: An old woman returns to her home village near Poitiers after a 40-year absence. Instead of the warm welcome she expected, she discovers that her brother has committed suicide and her sister-in-law has become an alcoholic. She endeavours to hold the family together for the sake of the children.

Comments: *Aunt Jeanne/Tante Jeanne* is another example in Simenon's work of conflict within a deeply dysfunctional family, with an attempted redemption.

The Girl in His Past/Le Temps d'Anaïs, 1951, translated by Louise Varèse

Plot: Albert Bauche has been married to Fernande for five years. He kills his rival Serge Nicolas, unaware that his wife was the man's mistress and had used her influence to get him his job.

Comments: Another treatment of a key Simenon theme: an individual trying to escape from an unsatisfying life. The reader gains a keen understanding of the criminal through an account of his past life.

A New Lease of Life/Une Vie Comme Neuve, 1951
(also translated as *A New Lease on Life*)

Plot: An unmarried 39-year-old accountant, Maurice Dudon, steals money from his boss to visit a certain Madame Germaine. One day he is knocked down in a road accident, and this changes his life. He attempts to make a completely new start, but the past soon catches up with him.

Comments: Obsessions die hard, and the wheel of fate comes full circle in this assured novel. The accountant Maurice is a fully fleshed, multifaceted creation.

The Girl with a Squint/Marie qui Louche, 1951, translated by Helen Thomson

Plot: The novel follows the lives of two childhood friends who try to escape from their poor backgrounds, and the action takes place between the years 1922 and 1950. Sylvie is the more reckless of the two and manages to establish a life of reasonable affluence. But Marie leads a quiet and reserved life with a modest job. After losing touch with each other for many years, the two friends decide to try living together again.

Comments: A novel that is characteristic of Simenon's interest in contrasting two completely different characters – a recurrent motif in his work.

Belle/La Mort de Belle, 1952, translated by Louise Varèse

Plot: Spencer Ashby, a history teacher in a market town in the USA, is accused of murdering a young girl who has been staying with him and his wife. He feels increasingly humiliated by the endless police interrogations and by his dismissal from the college. He begins to behave more and more like a guilty man, although he is in fact innocent. Completely demoralised, he begins to do things that are out of character, and eventually lives up to the suspicions that people have of him.

Comments: What is the extent of our potential criminality? This is the question posed in *Belle/La Mort de Belle*, a particularly mordant novel with its revelation of the incipient criminal within all of us.

The Brothers Rico/Les Frères Rico, 1952, translated by Ernst Pawel

Plot: The novel focuses on the three Rico brothers, who are members of the Mafia and who get involved in settling scores in a ruthless spiral of violence.

Comments: An atypical novel, memorable for its preoccupation entirely with the Mafia, strikingly characterised (albeit with a Gallic tint). *The Brothers Rico/Les Frères Rico* became well known through the celebrated US film version in 1958.

The Magician/Antoine et Julie, 1953, translated by Helen Sebba

Plot: Antoine, a conjuror, and Julie are married. But Antoine is an alcoholic. One evening, while he is out drinking, Julie has a sudden attack of angina. But it takes a further attack to disturb his conscience.

Comments: It has been noted by several commentators that the effects of alcohol on a relationship was a theme close to Simenon's heart, as communicated wryly to me by his UK editor, Christopher Sinclair-Stevenson.

The Iron Staircase/L'Escalier de Fer, 1953, translated by Eileen Ellenbogen

Plot: The novel begins in the bedroom of an apartment over a stationery suppliers where the fortyish Étienne muses on a recent heart attack. His wife Louise manages the shop, frequently ascending the eponymous spiral iron staircase to find out how Étienne is faring. What follows is as disturbing as it is unexpected.

Comments: An unsparing examination of a bourgeois marriage, *The Iron Staircase/L'Escalier de Fer* has echoes of Patricia Highsmith in its rigorous, coolly observed portrait of a relationship.

Red Lights/Feux Rouges, 1953, translated by Norman Denny

Plot: The protagonists, Steve, and his wife, Nancy, leave Long Island to collect their children from summer camp in Maine. But Steve is envious of Nancy's excellent job and resents her sarcasm. Alcohol accentuates his feelings of inadequacy. Then Nancy disappears…

Comments: A quotidian world of gas stations, diners and

rundown seaside towns is conjured with maximum vividness in an impressive novel.

The Fugitive/Crime Impuni, 1954 (also translated as *Account Unsettled*)

Plot: The novel starts in the 1920s in Liège with a young Polish student, Élie, who is in love with Louise, but who cannot stand the attentions paid her by the rich and handsome young Romanian Michel. One foggy night, Élie guns Michel down. The scene then changes to 25 years later in Arizona, when Élie meets the man he thought he had killed.

Comments: This is of particular interest because of the sharp contrasts between the characters of the two men, between two different periods, and between two completely different countries. In this novel, Simenon is once again more interested in the rigorous exploration of the characters' lives – in this case, Élie's – than in the exigencies of the crime novel. Another familiar theme is the stultifying nature of a mundane bourgeois existence.

The Watchmaker of Everton/L'Horloger d'Everton, 1954, translated by Norman Denny (also translated as *The Watchmaker* and *The Clockmaker*)

Plot: Dave Galloway, a watchmaker in a village in New York State, has been devoted to his son Ben since his wife left him. One night the 16-year-old Ben does not come home. Shortly afterwards, Dave is shocked to learn that his son is being sought by the police for murder. When his son is imprisoned he decides to help him, but Ben is indifferent to his interest and does not want to see his father. Despite the pain his son's attitude causes him, Dave identifies with his son and tries to understand him.

Comments: *The Watchmaker of Everton/L'Horloger d'Everton* is one of Simenon's most moving novels about the relationship between father and son, written with great sensitivity.

Big Bob/Le Grand Bob, 1954, translated by Eileen M. Lowe

Plot: A doctor tries to understand the death of a friend, 'Le Grand Bob', who seemed so happy and full of life. It is not clear at first whether the death was an accident or suicide.

Comments: *Big Bob/Le Grand Bob* is a poignant story with strikingly realised tragic elements.

The Witnesses/Les Témoins, 1955, translated by Moura Budberg

Plot: A magistrate at the court of assizes, Xavier Lhomond, has the job of investigating the soundness of the evidence against a man appearing before the court, and notices similarities with his own situation. He has a wife with cardiac problems, which forces him to be absent too often.

Comments: A subtle analysis of responsibility and guilt.

The Rules of the Game/La Boule Noire, 1955, translated by Howard Curtis

Plot: Connecticut businessman Walter Higgins is suffering a midlife crisis. Despite his comfortable lifestyle and affectionate family, he feels alienated from everything around him. What follows involves no specific crime, but it is equally life-changing for the protagonists.

Comments: Yet another demonstration of Simenon's sympathy for – and understanding of – the problems of a seemingly normal individual. The author is able to make minor catastrophes for his characters have the resonance of events on a far grander scale.

The Accomplices/Les Complices, 1956, translated by Bernard Frechtman

Plot: Joseph Lambert is responsible for a bad road accident, in which several children are killed. He is accompanied by his secretary, Edmonde, who is also his lover, when the accident happens and he decides to drive off and not give himself up to the police. He can be certain of Edmonde's silence, and is not particularly concerned at first, but gradually he becomes filled with remorse, and feels that there can be only one solution.

Comments: Less celebrated than it should be, *The Accomplices/ Les Complices* is a powerfully written, utterly convincing study of an individual who is racked by remorse.

In Case of Emergency/En Cas de Malheur, 1956, translated by Helen Sebba

Plot: Lucien Gobillot is a prominent defence lawyer who married the widow of his former boss and who moves in the best social circles. One day a young prostitute, Yvette, asks him to defend her and also offers herself to him. He fights off her advances at first but eventually gives in. He provides Yvette with her own apartment, but then learns that a spurned lover is threatening her. Tragedy ensues.

Comments: The novel is written in the form of a diary, a kind of secret report on the protagonist, or a 'dossier'. This means that the reader has the illusion of experiencing the events as they happen. One of the themes of the novel is that there are still so many unanswerable questions about people's motivations. A justly famous book, which was also made into a successful film.

The Little Man from Archangel/Le Petit Homme d'Arkhangelsk, 1956, translated by Siân Reynolds

Plot: Jonas Milk, a timid, 40-year-old bookseller and a Russian Jew, is living happily with his young wife, Gina, when one day she disappears. It seems likely that the young woman has gone off with a lover, but Jonas does not want to discuss the matter and is suspected of killing her.

Comments: *The Little Man from Archangel* persuasively presents the reader with the tale of a tragic miscarriage of justice and the overwhelming wave of memories it triggers of lost family, scattered during the traumatic events of the Russian Revolution.

The Son/Le Fils, 1957

Plot: On the death of his father, Alain Lefrançois starts telling his own 16-year-old son the story of his life. He is haunted by a secret that he shared with his father, who considered himself responsible for the death of Alain's pregnant girlfriend. In writing this confession to his son, he hopes to gain his son's understanding.

Comments: *The Son/Le Fils* is persuasive, especially as a study of the relationships between three generations of a family.

The Negro/Le Nègre, 1957, translated by Helen Sebba

Plot: The corpse of a black man is found one winter's morning by a railway embankment. It is suspected that he fell from the late-night train from Amiens, but Théo, the keeper of a small station nearby, saw the figure of the man, in full moonlight, going away from the embankment towards the village. It is obvious, therefore, that he met his death by some other means, but only Théo has knowledge of this evidence. The Cadieu brothers seem likely to be implicated in the affair, and Théo sees his chance to change his dreary life once and for all with the help of a little blackmail.

Comments: Critics have been sharply divided about this

work, some classing it as a minor work, others considering it a convincing psychological study of a man desperately trying to escape from a boring life in which he feels inferior to others.

The Premier/Le Président, 1958, translated by Daphne Woodward

Plot: A former *président du Conseil*, retired following an electoral defeat, is writing his memoirs in his clifftop home in Normandy. He dreams of returning to power through a government crisis. He has one hope: he has a hold over his former secretary, Chalamont, who is said to be forming the next government. Chalamont once betrayed him and the country, and the former premier still has the man's written confession. Will he do a deal?

Comments: It is unusual for Simenon to set a novel entirely in the world of politics, but his portrait of the ageing statesman desperately wanting to cling on to the influence he used to wield is very convincing.

Striptease/Strip-Tease, 1958, translated by Robert Brain

Plot: A group of strippers are employed by a low-rent Cannes nightclub, run by the husband-and-wife duo of Monsieur Léon and former prostitute Madame Florence. The ex-pimp Léon forces a new stripper into sex as a condition of employment. But Maud, the new arrival, is to bring about irrevocable change in the exploitative set-up.

Comments: A cool and unsentimental vision of lives lived at the very edge, with the hopeless aspirations of the strippers cruelly crushed. One of Simenon's most uncompromising novels.

Sunday/Dimanche, 1959, translated by Nigel Ryan

Plot: Émile is married to a domineering older wife. It is her family who own the inn, 'La Bastide', which they run together near Nice. Émile is the chef but feels like a servant. To assert his independence he takes a maid as his mistress, but he is still continually humiliated by his wife. Finally he hatches a plot to poison her, but he reckons without his wife's own ingenuity.

Comments: Although set on one day, the narrative concurrently reveals events from the past. It is a masterly study of a mind obsessed.

The Grandmother/La Vieille, 1959

Plot: A grandmother agrees to spend her last years with her granddaughter, a famous parachutist. Being very much alike, however, the two women are soon at loggerheads.

Comments: Unusual among Simenon's works for having two female protagonists. A riveting study of loneliness and the problems of communication.

The Widower/Le Veuf, 1959, translated by Robert Baldick

Plot: A 40-year-old man tries to understand why his wife has committed suicide alone in a Paris hotel room. Investigating her past, he discovers that she was keeping something secret from him.

Comments: *The Widower/Le Veuf* deals in authoritative fashion with the not uncommon habit among Simenon characters of leading a double life.

Teddy Bear/L'Ours en Peluche, 1960, translated by Henry Clay

Plot: A famous gynaecologist leads a dull family life, which he attempts to escape from through his relationship with his secretary, Viviane. He also has a brief affair with a woman called Emma, the 'Teddy Bear' of the title, but when she is rejected by the gynaecologist's circle she commits suicide. He becomes dominated by a sense of responsibility for Emma's death, and his despair eventually turns into aggression.

Comments: *Teddy Bear/L'Ours en Peluche* is a sombre and unremitting novel, but compelling and ingeniously written to the very end.

Betty/Betty, 1961, translated by Ros Schwartz

Plot: A young woman of 28, Élisabeth (Betty) Étamble, is forced to leave her husband by her in-laws, who consider her conduct to be scandalous. She escapes into a sleazy world of drug addicts and drunks, and finally takes refuge in a hotel with a doctor's widow called Laure Lavancher, in whom she confides everything. Laure's decision to help Betty has a tragic outcome.

Comments: A haunting story turned into a successful film by Claude Chabrol, a filmmaker who demonstrated a markedly similar ethos to Simenon, as mentioned elsewhere in this study.

The Train/Le Train, 1961, translated by Robert Baldick

Plot: Marcel Féron flees the German invasion in the spring of 1940 with his pregnant wife and four-year-old daughter. He becomes separated from his family while being evacuated by train. He meets a young Jewish girl, Anna, and they become lovers. When the train arrives in La Rochelle, Marcel and Anna meet again in a camp, but Marcel soon learns that his wife is not far away and has given birth. He decides to go back to his wife. But later, when he and his family are together again in the Ardennes, the Jewish girl reappears, needing his help.

Comments: The setting of the novel is utterly convincing and no doubt owes much to Simenon's own experiences of helping refugees during the war.

The Door/La Porte, 1962, translated by Daphne Woodward

Plot: Bernard, a war invalid, who has lost his hands, lives with his wife Nelly in Paris. One day he finds his wife in the arms of their neighbour, a young, handicapped man. This, not unnaturally, induces a severe emotional crisis in Bernard.

Comments: Simenon's work – frequently bleak – does not come much bleaker than this unsparing novel. One, perhaps, for aficionados rather than casual readers.

The Others/Les Autres, 1962, translated by Alastair Hamilton (also translated as *The House on Quai Notre Dame*)

Plot: A 40-year-old art teacher, Blaise Huet, is writing a journal. The death of an uncle and the unexpected return of a cousin lead him to reflect on his life.

Comments: *The Others/Les Autres* is a markedly concise novel, but it manages to reflect within its brevity the internecine conflicts within a provincial family.

The Patient/Les Anneaux de Bicêtre, 1963, translated by Jean Stewart (also translated as *The Bells of Bicêtre*)

Plot: A wealthy press mogul, René Maugras, is in the hospital at Bicêtre, after becoming unwell in a restaurant. He is paralysed but gradually regains contact with the world around him. He reviews his life, his successes and failures, and also his marriage to Lina, who has long been an alcoholic.

Comments: A familiar theme of a man in crisis reviewing his life, but this novel has an upbeat quality that makes it strangely uplifting.

The Blue Room/La Chambre Bleue, 1964, translated by Linda Coverdale

Plot: A self-regarding, womanising man and a sensuous but manipulative woman meet eight times in 11 months in the blue room of the Hôtel des Voyageurs, for erotically abandoned afternoons. But the sexual passion changes into something else when their long-term plans come into conflict. Soon, the hapless Tony is caught in the nightmare of a double murder.

Comments: *The Blue Room* is a concise masterpiece of psychological crime writing. After its initial publication, the book was fated to remain inexplicably out of print for over 35 years before a welcome reappearance. Wry and economical, the novel is a good entrée to Simenon's complex universe. The real strength of this novel is in the profound study of the psychology of the murderer, utterly convincing, and characteristic of some of the most accomplished *romans durs*.

The Man with the Little Dog/L'Homme au Petit Chien, 1964, translated by Jean Stewart

Plot: Félix Allard has come out of prison and leads a quiet life with the company of his little dog, expecting that he will die soon, as his doctor has predicted. He writes down an account of his life in a school exercise book, including a report on how he worked as a clerk, made some success of himself, and finally murdered his wife's lover.

Comments: For most readers the ending of this novel is a shock. It is simultaneously beautifully ironic.

The Little Saint/Le Petit Saint, 1965, translated by Bernard Frechtman

Plot: The novel traces the development of a painter, Louis Cuchas, and his art, and reveals how he remained faithful to his childhood experiences.

Comments: *The Little Saint/Le Petit Saint* is rare among Simenon's works in showing how a man raises himself above his environment and attains some measure of greatness.

The Venice Train/Le Train de Venise, 1965, translated by Ros Schwartz

Plot: Justin Calmar is asked by a stranger on board a train from Venice to deliver a briefcase to an address in Lausanne. He agrees, only to find that he is holding a fortune in currency, but has a corpse on his hands. He decides to keep the money but not tell his wife and family about it. His reward is only lies and fear.

Comments: The strength of *The Venice Train/Le Train de Venise* lies in its keen analysis of anxiety.

The Confessional/Le Confessionnal, 1966, translated by Jean Stewart

Plot: The story focuses on the completely dysfunctional family of a dentist. The constant disagreements between the parents cause great distress to the schoolboy son, André, who seeks comfort in the arms of a girl from a more stable background.

Comments: It has been claimed that the novel reflects many of the personal problems in Simenon's own family.

The Old Man Dies/La Mort d'Auguste, 1966, translated by Bernard Frechtman

Plot: When Auguste, the owner of a restaurant in Les Halles, Paris, dies, his three sons fight each other for their inheritance. A shock is in store for them.

Comments: A highly accomplished novel about a family dominated – and twisted – by selfish avarice.

The Cat/Le Chat, 1967, translated by Bernard Frechtman

Plot: After losing their spouses, Marguerite and Émile marry each other out of the need to avoid loneliness. But they begin to loathe each other. One day Émile's cat is poisoned and, suspecting Marguerite of having done it, Émile refuses to speak to her. From then on they only communicate through notes, although they discover that they cannot actually bring themselves to separate. The future is indeed bleak.

Comments: A very disturbing book, providing little comfort. Somehow a relationship survives on purely negative feelings. The couple is held together by their own emptiness. Brilliantly honest about a human relationship at its worst. Jean Gabin and Simone Signoret interpreted the characters with great conviction in the film version.

The Neighbours/Le Déménagement, 1967, translated by Christopher Sinclair-Stevenson (also translated as *The Move*)

Plot: The director of a Paris travel agency, Émile Jovis, leaves his apartment in the Rue des Francs-Bourgeois and moves to a modern apartment in the suburbs. But the walls are very thin, and he overhears the conversations of his new neighbour, who turns out to be the owner of a striptease club. This is a whole new sleazy world for Émile, and he becomes drawn into the clutches of a gang of crooks.

Comments: The novel is provocative for its contrast between traditional values and the amoral modern world.

The Prison/La Prison, 1968, translated by Lyn Moir

Plot: The wife of the director of a weekly magazine has killed her own sister. The director is mystified and tries to find out why she did it. The two sisters never liked each other, but there is something in their past that fired their common hatred.

Comments: The past rears its ugly head to rob the present of meaning and purpose. Yet another Simenon novel in which the central character discovers the pointlessness of his own existence.

The Hand/La Main, 1968, translated by Linda Coverdale (also translated as *The Man on the Bench in the Barn*)

Plot: Two couples returning from a reception in a snowbound Connecticut, USA, have to abandon their car, which gets stuck in a snowdrift. When they arrive at the house of Donald Dodd, it is discovered that one member of the group, Ray, has disappeared. Donald pretends to go off searching for him but in fact hides in the barn. Two days later Ray's body is found, but Donald does not consider himself responsible for his friend's death. Eventually Ray's widow becomes Donald's lover, but the affair ends tragically.

Comments: A novel written in the first person, a mode that Simenon handled with casual mastery; it is another attempt on the part of a murderer to understand his own behaviour. It is also a novel set entirely in the USA; but unlike others that feature an American setting, it was written many years after Simenon's actual stay there.

November/Novembre, 1969, translated by Jean Stewart

Plot: The usual dismal weather in November reflects the mood in the Le Cloanec family. Each member of the family lives in his or her own world: the mother is a drunkard, the father is sullenly absorbed in his work, and the children are struggling with their adolescent crises. A pretty young Spanish maid, Manuela, disturbs the household by dispensing her favours to the son, and eventually to the father. But one day Manuela disappears.

Comments: The novel is about a family that was heading for disaster in a variety of fashions; Manuela just happens to be the catalyst. Only one character, the daughter Laura, manages to rise above it all; she is also the narrator.

The Rich Man/Le Riche Homme, 1970, translated by Jean Stewart

Plot: Victor Lecoin, a prosperous mussel cultivator, lives in Marsilly and is envied by his neighbours as 'the rich man'. He is married to Jeanne, but indulges himself in various amorous adventures, which everybody knows about. He falls in a big way for their new maid Alice, but then Alice is found murdered.

Comments: A central theme of *The Rich Man/Le Riche Homme* is the short-lived nature of happiness.

The Disappearance of Odile/La Disparition d'Odile, 1971, translated by Lyn Moir

Plot: An 18-year-old girl, Odile Pointet, decides to leave her family house in Lausanne for Paris. In a letter to her brother she tells him she is contemplating suicide. He promptly sets out to find her. She meets up with a young medical student who saves her from a suicide attempt by using a tourniquet, and he gives her new hope.

Comments: This is a rare example of the saturnine writer allowing hope to be born in the midst of despair. All the more ironic, when one considers that his own daughter, Marie-Jo, would commit suicide only a few years later.

The Glass Cage/La Cage de Verre, 1971, translated by Antonia White

Plot: Émile Virieu, 44 years old, is a proof corrector at a printers and works in an office that is a kind of glass cage; this gives him a certain sense of security. But suddenly his world is turned upside down by his brother-in-law's suicide. Émile becomes emotionally unstable and cannot control his feelings, which has lethal effects.

Comments: *The Glass Cage/La Cage de Verre* traces the slow but sure progress from repression of all feelings to pathological behaviour.

The Innocents/Les Innocents, 1972, translated by Eileen Ellenbogen

Plot: Georges Célerin, a jeweller, has been living an apparently normal family life, but after his wife is accidentally run over and killed in the Rue Washington, it is revealed that she had been deceiving him for 18 years, and with someone he knew very well.

Comments: *The Innocents/Les Innocents* is the last of the *romans durs*, and although there are no new departures thematically – in fact, it returns to a favourite Simenon theme: the effect on others of the revelation that someone has been leading a double life – it is a masterly piece. The perfect finis to a superlative series.

Other Short Story Collections

The Little Doctor/Le Petit Docteur, 1943, translated by Jean Stewart

Contents: 'The Doctor's Hunch' ('Le Flair du Petit Docteur'); 'The Girl in Pale Blue' ('La Demoiselle en Bleu Pâle'); 'A Woman Screamed' ('Une Femme a Crié'); 'The Haunting of Monsieur Marbe' ('Le Fantôme de M. Marbe'); 'The Midwinter Marriage' ('Les Mariés du 1er Décembre'); 'The Corpse in the Kitchen Garden' ('La Mort Tombé du Ciel'); 'The Dutchman's Luck' ('La Bonne Fortune du Hollandais'); 'Popaul and his Negro' ('Le Passager et son Nègre'); 'The Trail of the Red-Haired Man' ('La Piste de l'Homme Roux'); 'The Disappearance of the Admiral' ('L'Amiral a Disparu'); 'The Communication Cord' ('La Sonnette d'Alarme'); 'Arsenic Hall' ('Le Château de l'Arsenic'); 'Death in a Department Store' ('L'Amoureux aux Pantoufles').

Comments: A collection of rather more light-hearted stories featuring Jean Dollett, the 'Little Doctor' of the title, who discovers he has a passion and a genius for investigation.

SIMENON ON SCREEN

The listings below (which are comprehensive, but not exhaustive) are divided into films based on Maigret novels and those based on *romans durs*, and each list is chronological by the year in which the films were first released. The original title is indicated first (in its original language, where possible) and the country of origin, together with the year of release. This is followed by the title of an English translation of the original work on which the film is based. The subsequent headings depend on the information available for each film, but include, as a rule, director, adaptation (which includes screenplay and dialogue), and main actors (some well-known French actors are known by their family names only). Further information and comments are added where relevant.

Much more than the Simenon novels discussed in this study, it has been a particularly challenging task tracking down many of the films listed below, only some of which have obtained official releases on disc, and in some cases I have had to rely on my notes on viewing the films from years ago. (I am grateful for several contributions by Howard Curtis for some of the films I have been unable to see.)

Only those films for which information can be verified through reliable sources have been included. The listings are therefore not complete. One film has been deliberately omitted, because it contains only a short sketch based on the

Maigret short story 'The Evidence of the Altar-Boy', among other sketches. The title of the film is *Brelan d'As*, directed by Henri Verneuil, with Michel Simon as Maigret. It was released in 1952.

Maigret on Film

It didn't take long for canny filmmakers to realise the great potential of Maigret as a recurring screen detective – not least for the fact that the books were already much loved by the time the first film adaptation appeared. The first actor to portray Maigret on screen was the celebrated Pierre Renoir in *Night at the Crossroads/La Nuit du Carrefour*. Apart from the nicely judged, understated performance by the actor, the film had another considerable advantage: it was directed in 1932 by the actor's brother, the great Jean Renoir (director of the masterly *La Règle du Jeu*). This was, in fact, a good year for screen Maigrets, as another important director, Julien Duvivier, cast Harry Baur as the detective in *La Tête d'un Homme*, a solid if rather steadily paced outing that nevertheless honoured Simenon's original conception.

Gallic screen Maigrets aside, the first English-language incarnation of the detective was delivered by one of Britain's greatest character actors, Charles Laughton, in *The Man on the Eiffel Tower*, an adaptation of the novel *A Man's Head/La Tête d'un Homme*. The supporting cast was shored up by a bushel of other reliable character stars: Franchot Tone, Burgess Meredith (who also co-directed the film with Laughton) and Wilfrid Hyde-White among them. As so often in his career, Laughton could not resist incorporating several of his larger-than-life mannerisms into his assumption of Maigret, with a theatricality some distance from the low-key characterisations of the novels. But few viewers would have complained at the time, given the sheer value for money that Laughton provided in the part.

France was to provide a series of Maigret films: three, in fact, in which the actor Albert Préjean capably played the inspector: *Picpus* (1943), *Cécile Est Morte* (1944) and *Les Caves du Majestic* (1945). But efficient though Préjean's performance was, there was one actor who was clearly born to play Maigret – or so French audiences would have assumed – the great Jean Gabin. Solidly built, middle-aged and projecting an aura of authority and reliability, Gabin was perfect casting in three films: *Maigret Tend un Piège* (1958), the less successful *Maigret et l'Affaire Saint-Fiacre* (1959) and *Maigret Voit Rouge* (1963), the weakest of the three, with Maigret up against some gangsters in a rather desultory fashion. Despite the inconsistencies of the films, one might have assumed that Gabin's casting would have pleased the detective's creator, but, as we shall see, the perfect screen Maigret – in Simenon's eyes – was to appear from another source. One other Maigret on film should be noted at this point: Heinz Rühmann (a very uncanonical-looking Maigret) in Alfred Weidenmann's *Maigret und sein größter Fall* in 1966. Its miscast lead aside, the film bore signs of its international co-production status, and while not a 'Euro-pudding' (to use the familiar dismissive term for compromised international co-productions in which the various elements fail to coalesce), it has its virtues, despite being one of the less memorable entries in the Maigret filmography.

La Nuit du Carrefour

France, 1932 (*Night at the Crossroads*).
Director: Jean Renoir.
Adaptation: Jean Renoir and Georges Simenon.
Main actors: Pierre Renoir (Maigret), Winna Winifried, Georges Koudria, Georges Térof, Dignimont, Lucie Vallat.

Comments: Among the director Jean Renoir's sound films, *La Nuit du Carrefour* is somewhat under-regarded, but a filmmaker from another generation, the *Nouvelle Vague* rebel Jean-Luc Godard, was an inordinate admirer and called it 'the only great French detective movie'. The Hungarian director Béla Tarr observed that his own Simenon film *The Man from London* (see below) was made under the spell of Renoir's film. There is no doubt that the latter deserves a much wider currency than it has enjoyed.

Le Chien Jaune

France, 1932 (*The Yellow Dog*).
Director: Jean Tarride.
Adaptation: Jean Tarride and Georges Simenon.
Main actors: Abel Tarride (Maigret), Rosine Deréan, Jane Loury, Rolla Norman, Anthony Gildès, Robert Le Vigan.

Comments: While efficiently played, Abel Tarride's Maigret in *Le Chien Jaune* remains one of the less distinctive iterations of the inspector to be put on film.

La Tête d'un Homme

France, 1933 (*A Man's Head*).

Director: Julian Duvivier.
Adaptation: Louis Delaprée, Julien Duvivier and Pierre Calmann.
Main actors: Harry Baur (Maigret), Valéry Inkijinoff, Gina Manès, Line Noro, Gaston Jacquet, Alexandre Rignault.

Comments: Inkijinoff and Simenon themselves had worked on an adaptation of the novel, which Simenon thought of producing himself, but this was not used by Julian Duvivier. Harry Baur's is a notably successful version of Maigret, with the actor conveying sensitively the empathy of the character.

Picpus

France, 1943 (*To Any Lengths*).
Director: Richard Pottier.
Adaptation: Jean-Paul Le Chanois.
Main actors: Albert Préjean (Maigret), Jean Tissier, Édouard Delmont, Juliette Faber, Guillaume de Sax, Noël Roquevert.

Comments: In the wave of Simenon adaptations that were controversially made during the German occupation of France, Richard Pottier's takes an unusual approach for Maigret films, eschewing the more serious aspects of earlier works and emphasising a light comedy ethos (perhaps unsurprising, given the black mood of the French population under the German heel).

Cécile Est Morte

France, 1944 (*Cécile Is Dead*).
Director: Maurice Tourneur.

Adaptation: Jean-Paul Le Chanois and Michel Duran.
Main actors: Albert Préjean (Maigret), Santa Relli, Germaine Kerjean, Luce Fabiole, Liliane Maigné, André Gabriello, André Reybaz.

Comments: These days, the son of director Maurice Tourneur, Jacques, is perhaps better known than his father for such imperishable films as *Out of the Past*. But Maurice Tourneur was a considerable talent himself, as this solidly made Simenon adaptation proves. The contribution of art director Guy de Gastyne is equally impressive, and the film's neglect may be partly down to the fact that it was another adaptation made during the benighted period of the German occupation.

Les Caves du Majestic

France, 1945 (*The Cellars of the Majestic*).
Director: Richard Pottier.
Adaptation: Charles Spaak.
Main actors: Albert Préjean (Maigret), André Gabriello, Suzy Prim, Jean Marchat, Denise Grey, Jacques Baumer, René Génin, Florelle.

The Man on the Eiffel Tower

USA, 1949 (*A Man's Head*).
Director: Burgess Meredith.
Adaptation: Harry Brown and John Cortez.
Main actors: Charles Laughton (Maigret), Franchot Tone, Burgess Meredith, Robert Hutton, Jean Wallace, Patricia Roc, Belita, George Thorpe, William Phipps, William Cottrell, Chaz Chase, Wilfrid Hyde-White, Howard Vernon.

Comments: This version of Simenon's popular novel had a troubled production history, including such problems as the film's star Charles Laughton threatening to walk off the picture over a variety of disagreements with the director Irving Allen (who left the film and was replaced as director by Laughton's fellow actor Burgess Meredith). Unusually for a film with the scene-stealing British actor, Laughton is on less than impressive form here, and gives a rather underpowered performance; Franchot Tone (as a suspect) is more watchable.

Maigret Dirige l'Enquête

UK/France, 1956 (based on various works — see comment below).
Director: Stany Cordier.
Main actors: Maurice Manson (Maigret), Svetlana Pitoëff, Peter Walker, Michel André.

Comments: *Maigret Dirige l'Enquête* is one of the mysteries of cinematic history. It is a film that is rarely shown, and one critic who viewed it in 1979 was not able to come to any firm conclusions about it. It seems to be a British film, but it was filmed in Paris for the exterior shots. The actor, named in the credits as Maurice Manson, who plays Maigret, looks uncannily like Georges Simenon. Generally, the film is considered something of a disaster, but it has novelty value. It consists of several sketches based loosely on three Maigret works: *Cécile Is Dead*, *Death of a Nobody* and *Maigret and the Tall Woman*.

Maigret Tend un Piège

France, 1958 (*Maigret Sets a Trap*).

Director: Jean Delannoy.
Adaptation: Rodolphe-Maurice Arlaud, Michel Audiard and Jean Delannoy.
Main actors: Jean Gabin (Maigret), Annie Girardot, Jean Desailly, Jeanne Boitel, Gérard Séty, Lucienne Bogaërt, Jean Debucourt, Olivier Hussenot, Lino Ventura.

Comments: Generally considered to be one of the most creative and fully achieved versions of Simenon's work on film. As Howard Curtis noted when we discussed it, *Maigret Tend un Piège* is the first and best of Jean Gabin's three incarnations as Maigret. The film also boasts powerful supporting performances by Jean Desailly and Annie Girardot. It positively drips with Parisian atmosphere – in part due to the haunting theme music by Paul Misraki – although, as was common in French cinema of this period, its Paris is scrupulously recreated in the studio.

Maigret et l'Affaire Saint-Fiacre

France, 1959 (*The Saint-Fiacre Affair*).
Director: Jean Delannoy.
Adaptation: Rodolphe-Maurice Arlaud, Jean Delannoy and Michel Audiard.
Main actors: Jean Gabin (Maigret), Valentine Tessier, Michel Auclair, Michel Vitold, Robert Hirsch, Paul Frankeur, Jacques Morel, Armande Navarre.

Comments: When the Young Turks of the French *Nouvelle Vague* began taking potshots at an earlier generation of filmmakers (who they planned to supplant), there were several directors who were dismissed by the new young talents as fusty members of the 'Cinéma du Papa', out-of-date figures. One egregious casualty was the director Jean Delannoy, whose dismissal was particularly unjust, as this solid Simenon adaptation proves. A reassessment of the film by critic Jacques Lacourcelles went some way to restoring the reputation of the director, with Jean Gabin on fine form as the inspector visiting the town where he grew up.

Maigret Voit Rouge

France, 1963 (*Maigret, Lognon and the Gangsters*).
Director: Gilles Grangier.
Adaptation: Jacques Robert and Gilles Grangier.
Main actors: Jean Gabin (Maigret), Françoise Fabian, Vittorio Sanipoli, Paul Carpenter, Ricky Cooper, Michel Constantin, Paul Frankeur, Harry-Max, Guy Decomble.

Maigret und sein größter Fall

Germany, 1966 (*The Dancer at the Gai-Moulin*).
Director: Alfred Weidenmann.
Adaptation: Herbert Reinecker.
Main actors: Heinz Rühmann (Maigret), Françoise Prévost, Günther Stoll, Günter Strack, Gerd Vespermann, Eddi Arent, Günther Ungeheuer, Alexander Kerst, Ulli Lommel.

Comments: As well as appearing in the long-running British television series, Rupert Davies might have played Maigret in this adaptation, which hardly lives up to the translation of the title as 'Maigret's Greatest Case'. After Davies left over script disagreements, Heinz Rühmann took over as the inspector, delivering a rather bland and characterless performance. The final effect of the film is that of a workaday effort.

Maigret a Pigalle

Italy, 1967 (*Maigret at Picratt's*).
Director: Mario Landi.
Adaptation: Sergio Amidei and Mario Landi.
Main actors: Gino Cervi (Maigret), Lila Kedrova, Raymond Pellegrin, Alfred Adam, Christian Barbier, José Greci, Daniel Ollier, Enzo Cerusico.

Comments: This is a film version made as a spin-off from the long-running Italian TV series starring Gino Cervi. The first episode was also called *Maigret a Pigalle* and was broadcast in 1962. Some 36 episodes were planned for the series.

Maigret

France, 2022 (*Maigret and the Dead Girl*).
Director: Patrice Leconte.
Adaptation: Patrice Leconte and Jérôme Tonnerre.
Main actors: Gérard Depardieu, Jade Labeste, Aurore Clément, Mélanie Bernier.

Romans Durs on Film

Dernier Refuge

France, 1940 (*The Lodger*).
Director: Jacques Constant.
Adaptation: Jacques Constant and André-Paul Antoine.
Main actors: Mireille Balin, Georges Rigaud, Marie Glory,

Marcel Dalio, Saturnin Fabre, Mila Parély, Jean Tissier, Christian Argentin, Roger Blin.

Comments: This film is no longer available. Filming was apparently started in August 1939 at the Studios Saint-Maurice, but was interrupted after three weeks because of the declaration of war on 3 September. It continued eventually, and the production was finished in April 1940. The original negatives of the film were destroyed during a laboratory fire.

Annette et la Dame Blonde

France, 1942 (based on a short story published in the collection *La Rue aux Trois Poussins*, 1963 (not translated into English)).
Director: Jean Dréville.
Adaptation: Henri Decoin and Michel Duran.
Main actors: Louise Carletti, Henri Garat, Georges Rollin, Mona Goya, Simone Valère, Rosine Luguet, Marcelle Rexiane.

La Maison des Sept Jeunes Filles

France, 1942 (based on a 1941 novel of the same name (not translated into English)).
Director: Albert Valentin.
Adaptation: Jacques Viot, Maurice Blondeau and Charles Spaak.
Main actors: André Brunot, Jean Tissier, Jean Pâqui, Jean Rigaux, Marguerite Deval, René Bergeron, Paul Demange. The seven young girls were played by Gaby Andreu, Geneviève Beau, Jacqueline Bouvier, Josette Daydé, Solange Delporte, Marianne Hardy and Primerose Perret.

Les Inconnus dans la Maison

France, 1942 (*The Strangers in the House*).
Director: Henri Decoin.
Adaptation: Henri-Georges Clouzot.
Main actors: Raimu, Juliette Faber, Gabrielle Fontan, Jacques Baumer, Héléna Manson, Jean Tissier, Lucien Coëdel.

Comments: Not for the first time in discussions concerning the work of Simenon, issues of anti-Semitism were raised regarding the film *Les Inconnus dans la Maison*. The actor Marcel Mouloudji played a character who was initially called 'Ephraïm Luska'. Subsequent to the initial release in 1942, when the film was banned for its perceived anti-Semitic content after the war, re-release prints removed any indication that the character was Jewish, with his name re-voiced as Amédé (except for one occasion in a trial scene where the actor Raimu still uses the original name). These issues aside, the film is a more than respectable entry in the Simenon filmic canon. Apparently Joseph Losey refused to do a remake in 1963, because of what he described as a disastrous adaptation by George Tabori.

Monsieur La Souris

France, 1942 (*Monsieur La Souris*).
Director: Georges Lacombe.
Adaptation: Marcel Achard.
Main actors: Raimu, Aimé Clariond, Charles Granval, Micheline Francey, Raymond Aimos, Pierre Jourdan, Gilbert Gil, Marie Carlot.

Comments: This efficient adaptation was apparently the first film based on a Simenon novel to be released in the USA, under the title *Midnight in Paris*.

Le Voyager de la Toussaint

France, 1943 (*Strange Inheritance*).
Director: Louis Daquin.
Adaptation: Marcel Aymé and Louis Daquin.
Main actors: Assia Noris, Jules Berry, Gabrielle Dorziat, Guillaume de Sax, Roger Karl, Louis Seigner, Alexandre Rignault.

Comments: Apparently, if the viewer remains alert, it is possible to spot Simone Signoret among the extras.

L'Homme de Londres

France, 1943 (*The Man from London*).
Director: Henri Decoin.
Adaptation: Henri Decoin and Charles Exbrayat.
Main actors: Fernand Ledoux, Jules Berry, Suzy Prim, Héléna Manson, Blanche Montel, Jean Brochard, Mony Dalmès.

Panique

France, 1947 (*Mr Hire's Engagement*).
Director: Julien Duvivier.
Adaptation: Charles Spaak and Julien Duvivier.
Main actors: Michel Simon, Viviane Romance, Paul Bernard, Charles Dorat, Max Dalban, Magdeleine Gidon, Lucas Gridoux.

Comments: Julien Duvivier's *Panique* is another film that belongs in the first rank of Simenon adaptations, with direction and acting of a rare order. As Howard Curtis said to me: '*Panique* is one of the finest works by one of the most important French directors.' This film boasts a riveting central performance, at once creepy and sympathetic, by Michel Simon, a great actor who specialised in offbeat roles. Coming so soon after the occupation, its sour portrait of a community turning against an outsider (a frequent theme in Simenon) may have hit a nerve, accounting for its initial frosty reception, but it is now recognised as a masterpiece of the period. Fascinating to compare with Patrice Leconte's *Monsieur Hire*, a much later adaptation of the same source novel.

Dernier Refuge

France, 1947 (*The Lodger*).
Director: Marc Maurette.
Adaptation: Marc Maurette and Maurice Griffe.
Main actors: Raymond Rouleau, Mila Parély, Gisèle Pascal, Jean-Max, Marcel Carpentier, Noël Roquevert, Tramel.

Temptation Harbour

UK, 1947 (*The Man from London*).
Director: Lance Comfort.
Adaptation: Victor Skutezky, Fritz Gottfurcht (as Frederick Gotfurt) and Rodney Ackland.
Main actors: Robert Newton, Simone Simon, William Hartnell, Marcel Dalio, Margaret Barton, Edward Rigby, Joan Hopkins, Charles Victor, Kathleen Harrison, Irene Handl.

Comments: In the peculiar subgenre of British film noir — with production values less upholstered than those in the corresponding American product — a concomitant gain can be found in the unglamorous treatment of lives lived in quiet desperation. This is very much the case here, with the Gallic accoutrements of the original Simenon novel effectively transformed into a British setting (although the presence of Simone Simon, the star of Jacques Tourneur's *Cat People*, lends a French touch). Robert Newton, an actor well known for his scenery-chewing performances, is more restrained than usual here.

La Marie du Port

France, 1950 (*Chit of a Girl*).
Director: Marcel Carné.
Adaptation: Louis Chavance, Marcel Carné and Georges Ribemont-Dessaignes.
Main actors: Jean Gabin, Nicole Courcel, Blanchette Brunoy, Claude Romain, Julien Carette, Jane Marken, Georges Vitray.

Comments: It is reported that the writer Jacques Prévert worked on the design of the film, but this was not officially acknowledged. Rumours circulated for several years about plans for the film, and for a long time it was assumed that it would be directed by Pierre Billon, with the artist Maurice de Vlaminck designing the decor. That would have been an interesting choice, as Vlaminck was a close personal friend of Simenon.

Midnight Episode

USA, 1950 (*Monsieur La Souris*).

Director: Gordon Parry.

Adaptation: Rita Barisse, Reeve Tyler, Paul Vincent Carroll, David Evans and William Templeton.

Main actors: Stanley Holloway, Leslie Dwyer, Reginald Tate, Meredith Edwards, Wilfrid Hyde-White, Joy Shelton, Natasha Parry, Raymond Young, Leslie Perrins, Sebastian Cabot.

La Vérité sur Bébé Donge

France, 1952 (*The Trial of Bébé Donge*).

Director: Henri Decoin.

Adaptation: Maurice Aubergé.

Main actors: Danielle Darrieux, Jean Gabin, Daniel Lecourtois, Claude Génia, Gabrielle Dorziat, Jacqueline Porel, Jacques Castelot.

Comments: *La Vérité sur Bébé Donge* is not the most faithful of Simenon adaptations, but with two sacred monsters of French cinema in the main roles, the story's portrayal of a troubled marriage comes across as powerfully as in the source novel.

Le Fruit Défendu

France, 1952 (*Act of Passion*).

Director: Henri Verneuil.

Adaptation: Jacques Companéez, Jean Manse and Henri Verneuil.

Main actors: Fernandel, Sylvie, Françoise Arnoul, Claude Nollier, Jacques Castelot, Raymond Pellegrin, René Génin.

Comments: It was a brave decision indeed to cast the famous comic actor Fernandel as an obsessed murderer in *Le Fruit Défendu*. The resulting film is only fitfully successful, despite Henri Verneuil's best efforts.

The Man Who Watched the Trains Go By

USA, 1953 (*The Man Who Watched the Trains Go By*).
Director: Harold French.
Adaptation: Harold French and Paul Jarrico (originally uncredited).
Main actors: Claude Rains, Märta Torén, Marius Goring, Herbert Lom, Anouk Aimée, Lucie Mannheim, Felix Aylmer, Eric Pohlmann, Ferdy Mayne.

Comments: The film is said to have been offered to Joseph Losey but then he was put on the anti-communist blacklist and had to leave Hollywood. Claude Rains, one of the best character actors that the British Isles ever produced, is perfectly cast as Simenon's doomed protagonist, with strong support from the likes of Marius Goring, Herbert Lom, Anouk Aimée and Felix Aylmer.

La Neige Était Sale

France, 1954 (*The Snow Was Dirty*).
Director: Luis Saslavsky.
Adaptation: Luis Saslavsky and André Tabet.
Main actors: Daniel Gélin, Valentine Tessier, Marie Mansart, Daniel Ivernel, Véra Norman, Nadine Basile, Joëlle Bernard, Antoine Balpêtré.

A Life in the Balance
USA, 1955 ('Seven Little Crosses in a Notebook' in *Maigret's Christmas*).
Director: Harry Horner and Rafael Portillo (co-director).
Adaptation: Robert Presnell Jr and Leo Townsend.
Main actors: Ricardo Montalban, Anne Bancroft, Lee Marvin, José Pérez, Rodolfo Acosta, Carlos Múzquiz, Jorge Treviño.

The Bottom of the Bottle
USA, 1955 (*The Bottom of the Bottle*).
Director: Henry Hathaway.
Adaptation: Sydney Boehm.
Main actors: Van Johnson, Joseph Cotten, Ruth Roman, Jack Carson, Bruce Bennett, Brad Dexter, Peggy Knudsen, Jim Davis.

Comments: Non-French attempts at filming the novels of Simenon have been hit and miss, and director Henry Hathaway's *The Bottom of the Bottle* is something of a curate's egg, but it has undoubted plus points. Hathaway, one of Hollywood's most reliable professionals, put together an intriguing picture of family conflict with clashes between very disparate siblings to the fore. If Van Johnson (as an alcoholic on the run who has previously killed a man in a barroom fight) and Joseph Cotten (as an upscale solicitor) are encouraged to give unmodulated performances, the usually bland Ruth Roman is on top form as an embittered wife. There is also a strong supporting cast including Bruce Bennett, Pedro Gonzalez and Jack Carson. The Tucson, Arizona settings are some distance from Simenon's usual stamping grounds, but the final result is a diverting take on a key non-Maigret novel.

Le Sang à la Tête

France, 1956 (*Young Cardinaud*).
Director: Gilles Grangier.
Adaptation: Gilles Grangier and Michel Audiard.
Main actors: Jean Gabin, Paul Frankeur, Renée Faure, Monique Mélinand, José Quaglio, Claude Sylvain, Georgette Anys.

Le Passager Clandestin

France, 1958 (*The Stowaway*).
Director: Ralph Habib.
Adaptation: Maurice Aubergé, Ralph Habib and Paul Andréota.
Main actors: Martine Carol, Karlheinz Böhm, Arletty, Serge Reggiani, Roger Livesey, Reg Lye, Maëa Flohr.

Comments: It would appear that this was an international co-production, as it is credited to Discifilm and Silver Film in Paris, but also to Southern Films International, Sydney. The list of actors is also truly international, including, among others, French, German, Italian and British names.

The Brothers Rico

USA, 1958 (*The Brothers Rico*).
Director: Phil Karlson.
Adaptation: Lewis Meltzer, Ben Perry and Dalton Trumbo (uncredited – he was blacklisted at the time).
Main actors: Richard Conte, Dianne Foster, Kathryn Grant, Lamont Johnson, Larry Gates, James Darren, Paul Picerni, Argentina Brunetti.

Comments: The American director Phil Karlson was most celebrated for films in which a single individual is up against an insidiously powerful criminal organisation (it was a theme he explored from such films as *The Phenix City Story* (1955) right up to *Walking Tall* (1973)), but its most thorough iteration — and possibly the director's best film — was this adaptation of Simenon's novel. The first thing that is striking about the film is how discreet it is in terms of its violence; after an early beating, Karlson concentrates on building an atmosphere of mounting dread as he approaches the final explosive shootout, the latter more graphic than most films of the era. But the suspense for the characters – and the audience – is maintained through the sense that the Mafia (not so named in the film, but clearly identified as 'The Organisation') are up against one of their own – albeit a reluctant opponent, an ex-accountant played by the excellent Richard Conte. Eddie Rico is a low-level employee, never involved in violence, who has retired from the mob to run a successful legit business. But he is reluctantly drawn in again when his brother Johnny is forced into hiding after his part in a gangland killing, along with another Rico brother. The naive Eddie is persuaded by the seemingly amiable Capo Sid Kubik to find his brother in order to persuade him to go into hiding, but the viewer is quickly aware that his real job is to finger his brother for elimination. The film develops a nicely Kafkaesque sense that there is no place that is safe – every move that Eddie makes, every phone call, and every hotel he stays in is quickly identified by the mob, and the final murderous result is grimly inevitable. As so often with film adaptations, changes were made to the novel – in Simenon's book, the Rico character painfully persuades himself that the mob is right, and that summary justice must be dispensed, but this solution would not have been possible in the Hollywood of the day (the rather arbitrarily tacked-on happy ending also reveals the change to the plot). However, the steadily mounting nightmare is handled with tremendous assurance, and Conte is called upon to do far more than he customarily is – particularly in the wrenching scenes when he realises that his entire life, as well as his recent actions, has been built on compromise and betrayal. In the pantheon of films made from Simenon novels, this is one of the best. There was a television remake in 1972, entitled *The Family Rico*, directed by Paul Wendkos, and starring Ben Gazzara, James Farentino, Jo Van Fleet, Dane Clark and John Marley.

En Cas de Malheur

France, 1958 (*In Case of Emergency*).
Director: Claude Autant-Lara.
Adaptation: Jean Aurenche and Pierre Bost.
Main actors: Jean Gabin, Brigitte Bardot, Edwige Feuillère, Nicole Berger, Franco Interlenghi, Madeleine Barbulée, Julien Bertheau.

Comments: *En Cas de Malheur* was renamed in catchpenny fashion as *Love is My Profession* in English-speaking countries, with the film sold very much on Bardot's sex appeal. A somewhat stagey adaptation from the reliable if uninspired Autant-Lara, but Gabin is as impressive as ever as the middle-aged lawyer who falls for the charms of his young client. A much seen still of Bardot hitching up her skirt to her waist to entice Gabon had a notable effect on the film's reputation.

Le Baron de l'Écluse

France, 1959 (based on a short story published in the collection *Le Bateau d'Émile*, 1954).

Director: Jean Delannoy.

Adaptation: Maurice Druon, Jean Delannoy and Michel Audiard.

Main actors: Jean Gabin, Micheline Presle, Blanchette Brunoy, Jean Desailly, Jacques Castelot, Jean Constantin, Aimée Mortimer.

Comments: Gentle, elegant and sophisticated French comedies were relatively rare in the 1960s, and there were many who welcomed Jean Delannoy's *Le Baron de l'Écluse* with open arms. Admittedly, this Simenon-derived piece (something of a rarity in the twenty-first century) never achieves any more than a superficial grip, but it is accomplished enough to be constantly engrossing. Jean Gabin excels as a well mannered, likeable old fraud who makes a living by trying his luck at the tables or scrounging.

Le Président

France, 1961 (*The Premier*).

Director: Henri Verneuil.

Adaptation: Henri Verneuil and Michel Audiard.

Main actors: Jean Gabin, Bernard Blier, Renée Faure, Alfred Adam, Louis Seigner, Henri Crémieux, Robert Vattier, Charles Cullum.

La Mort de Belle

France, 1961 (*Belle*).

Director: Édouard Molinaro.

Adaptation: Jean Anouilh, Édouard Molinaro and Pierre Kast (uncredited).

Main actors: Jean Desailly, Monique Mélinand, Alexandra Stewart, Jacques Monod, Yvette Etiévant, Marc Cassot.

Comments: Of particular note in this production is the collaboration with Jean Anouilh, one of France's most prominent and original playwrights. The director Édouard Molinaro, perhaps best known (to his displeasure) for such comic outings as *La Cage au Folles*, shows that he has the measure of the material.

Le Bateau d'Émile

France, 1962 (based on a short story published in the collection *Le Bateau d'Émile*, 1954).

Director: Denys de La Patellière.

Adaptation: Denys de La Patellière, Albert Valentin and Michel Audiard.

Main actors: Annie Girardot, Lino Ventura, Pierre Brasseur, Michel Simon, Jacques Monod, Edith Scob, Joëlle Bernard.

L'Aîné des Ferchaux

France, 1963 (*The First-Born*).

Director: Jean-Pierre Melville.

Adaptation: Jean-Pierre Melville.

Main actors: Jean-Paul Belmondo, Charles Vanel, Michèle Mercier, Malvina Silberberg, Stefania Sandrelli, Andrex, Todd Martin.

Comments: A film version of the novel had been planned in 1961 by Jean Valère and was to star Michel Simon, Alain Delon and Romy Schneider. This version is serviceable.

Trois Chambres à Manhattan
France, 1965 (*Three Bedrooms in Manhattan*).
Director: Marcel Carné.
Adaptation: Marcel Carné and Jacques Sigurd.
Main actors: Annie Girardot, Maurice Ronet, Roland Lesaffre, Otto E. Hasse, Gabriele Ferzetti, Geneviève Page, Robert Hoffmann, Margaret Nolan, Virginia Lee.

Comments: For her performance, Annie Girardot received the Volpi Cup for actresses at the Venice Film Festival in 1965. Before giving her the role, Carné had also considered Simone Signoret and Jeanne Moreau. Jean Renoir had considered filming the novel in 1957 with Leslie Caron. Jean Pierre Melville also planned to film it with Monica Vitti. A film trivia note: a very young Robert De Niro can be spotted in the background of a bar scene.

Stranger in the House
USA/UK, 1967, also known as *Cop-Out* (*The Strangers in the House*).
Director: Pierre Rouve.
Adaptation: Pierre Rouve.
Main actors: James Mason, Geraldine Chaplin, Bobby Darin, Paul Bertoya, Ian Ogilvy, Bryan Stanyon [Stanion], Pippa Steel, Clive Morton, James Hayter, Megs Jenkins, Marjie Lawrence, Moira Lister.

Comments: The selling point for this adaptation of a previously filmed Simenon novel is the presence of the always reliable James Mason as the alcoholic solicitor Sawyer, a man adrift after the fragmentation of his family. But Mason's performance is not matched by that of his colleagues, with Geraldine Chaplin and Bobby Darin both ill at ease in their roles. Mason apart, admirers of the novel may find their time better occupied by picking up the original. This was a Dimitri De Grunwald production but distributed by the UK company Rank.

Le Chat

France, 1971 (*The Cat*).
Director: Pierre Granier-Deferre.
Adaptation: Pierre Granier-Deferre and Pascal Jardin.
Main actors: Jean Gabin, Simone Signoret, Annie Cordy, Jacques Rispal, Nicole Desailly, Harry-Max, André Rouyer, Carlo Nell, Yves Barsacq.

Comments: A bleak, disturbing film that captures well the atmosphere of the novel. For some inexplicable reason the names of the main characters were changed. Émile and Marguerite have become Julien and Clémence.

La Veuve Couderc

France, 1971 (*Ticket of Leave*).
Director: Pierre Granier-Deferre.
Adaptation: Pierre Granier-Deferre and Pascal Jardin.
Main actors: Simone Signoret, Alain Delon, Ottavia Piccolo, Jean Tissier, Monique Chaumette, Boby Lapointe.

Comments: *La Veuve Couderc* is Pierre Granier-Deferre's second Simenon adaptation (after *Le Chat*), and he takes some liberties with the source novel, but Delon and Signoret are both impressive. A solid star vehicle of its time.

Le Train

France, 1973 (*The Train*).
Director: Pierre Granier-Deferre.
Adaptation: Pierre-Graniere and Pascal Jardin.
Main actors: Jean-Louis Trintignant, Romy Schneider, Régine, Maurice Biraud, Nike Arrighi, Franco Mazzieri, Serge Marquand.

Comments: For his third Simenon adaptation, Pierre Granier-Deferre tackles one of Simenon's most unusual and powerful novels, set against the background of the German invasion of France in 1940. The wartime setting is recreated in hallucinatory detail, as it is in the novel, and Trintignant and Schneider are moving as the lovers thrown together by circumstances. The film adds a note of redemption at the end that is absent from the bleak original.

L'Horloger de Saint-Paul

France, 1974 (*The Watchmaker of Everton*).
Director: Bertrand Tavernier.
Adaptation: Jean Aurenche, Pierre Bost and Bertrand Tavernier.
Main actors: Philippe Noiret, Jean Rochefort, Jacques Denis, Julien Bertheau, Sylvain Rougerie, Cécile Vassort, Christine Pascal.

Comments: *L'Horloger de Saint-Paul* is the debut film of the director Bertrand Tavernier, and it is more conventional in form than the filmmaker's subsequent work. Nevertheless, this approach works well in terms of realising Simenon's novel. The book – with its minimalist plot – is a difficult one to adapt to another medium, but Philippe Noiret is as adept as ever at conveying the inner life of his character, Michel, coming to terms with the behaviour of his son. The film obtained the Prix Louis Delluc, and it is sensitive and well acted, but purists will find very little of Simenon's sharp dialogue remaining.

Der Mörder

Germany, 1979 (*The Murderer*).
Director: Ottokar Runze.
Adaptation: Ottokar Runze.
Main actors: Gerhard Olschewski, Johanna Liebeneiner, Marius Müller-Westernhagen, Wolfgang Wahl, Uta Hallant.

L'Étoile du Nord

France, 1982 (*The Lodger*).
Director: Pierre Granier-Deferre.
Adaptation: Jean Aurenche, Michel Grisolia and Pierre Granier-Deferre.
Main actors: Simone Signoret, Philippe Noiret, Fanny Cottençon, Julie Jézéquel, Jean Rougerie, Jean-Pierre Klein, Jean-Yves Chatelais.

Les Fantômes du Chapelier

France, 1982 (*The Hatter's Ghosts*).
Director: Claude Chabrol.

Adaptation: Claude Chabrol.

Main actors: Michel Serrault, Charles Aznavour, Aurore Clément, Monique Chaumette, Isabelle Sadoyan.

Comments: Of particular note here is director Claude Chabrol's cool and compelling take on Simenon. While other directors of the French New Wave fell by the wayside, Chabrol consolidated his career longevity by making crime-oriented cinema his special preserve. Apart from noting that the music is by Matthieu Chabrol, it is worth pointing out that a song used in the film was written by Charles Aznavour, who also plays (effectively) the role of the nervous tailor, Kachoudas.

Équateur

France, 1983 (*Tropic Moon*).

Director: Serge Gainsbourg.

Adaptation: Serge Gainsbourg.

Main actors: Barbara Sukowa, Francis Huster, Reinhard Kolldehoff, François Dyrek, Jean Bouise, Julien Guiomar, Roland Blanche, Murray Gronwall.

Comments: Most of the filming of *Équateur* was done in the republic of Gabon, West Africa. The music was also provided by the director.

Monsieur Hire

France, 1989 (*Mr Hire's Engagement*).

Director: Patrice Leconte.

Adaptation: Patrice Leconte and Patrick Dewolf.

Main actors: Michel Blanc, Sandrine Bonnaire, André Wilms, Luc Thuillier, Eric Bérenger, Marielle Berthon.

Comments: *Monsieur Hire* is a notably unusual Simenon adaptation with its rigorously observed portrait of a solitary, alienated man without friends. His neighbours distrust him, so it is no surprise when, after the murder of a woman, they consider that this unprepossessing man is responsible. With its startling plot turns, Patrice Leconte's adaptation creates and maintains a deeply unsettling atmosphere.

Betty

France, 1992 (*Betty*).
Director: Claude Chabrol.
Adaptation: Claude Chabrol.
Main actors: Marie Trintignant, Stéphane Audran, Jean-François Garreaud, Yves Lambrecht, Christiane Minazzoli.

Comments: After a variety of misfires, the great French filmmaker Claude Chabrol turned again to one of his favourite writers for source material. The film is a Chabrol family affair: Thomas Chabrol is featured as an actor; the original music was by Matthieu Chabrol; and the script supervisor was Aurore Chabrol. Marie Trintignant provides a stunningly vulnerable performance as the maltreated young woman whose life has been cast adrift before she is (seemingly) rescued from a desperate existence by an enigmatic and soignée older woman played by the director's muse – and wife – Stéphane Audran.

Chabrol, one of the leading lights of the late 1950s/early 1960s *Nouvelle Vague* movement, had expressed an affection for *Four Days in a Lifetime/Les Quatre Jours du Pauvre Homme*, which he called 'a very beautiful book', but never filmed it. He also noted (in *Claude Chabrol: Interviews*, edited by Christopher Beach): 'Simenon is pretty fast reading – each book averages about 160 pages – so as you finish one, you immediately start reading another. I had therefore read three or four in a row. I fell upon *Betty*, which I had read in the past. I heard about the book again when, coincidentally, I met Marc, Simenon's eldest son, who recommended that I read it, not knowing that I had already read it. Re-reading it, I literally fell in love with the girl. I immediately wanted to live with that girl for two or three months. That is how I decided to make the film. Next, I spoke to the producer, who was Marin Karmitz, and with whom I have a close relationship. I asked him which of my two projects – *Betty* or another one that interested me – he preferred. He answered: "Do the more impossible one: *Betty*." I informed him that the rights were available and he asked me when I wanted to start shooting. He came up with a generous budget, and, *voila!*, we were on the road. It was as banal and simple as that!'

The resulting film is one of the director's most successful. Such films as *Les Biches*, *Que la Bête Meure* and *La Femme Infidèle* showed the French director in Hitchcockian territory, a favourite stamping ground: murder, moral ambiguity and quiet desperation all tear apart the surfaces of the comfortable middle-class settings. With *Betty*, a cool and compelling take on Simenon, the director has the full measure of a remarkable novel. As with the original, we are given a penetrating psychological study, but, as so often with Chabrol, no easy answers are afforded for the questions raised. The director's earlier adaptation of a Simenon novel, *Les Fantômes du Chapelier*, had underlined the similar world view of the two artists – writer and filmmaker – both of whom were more prolific in their respective outputs than most of their peers. But the principal thing they shared was a sort of cool Olympian detachment from their characters, with the audience invited to view events *sub specie aeternitatis* – decidedly from a distance and searching for timeless verities. Marie Trintignant gives a remarkable, fragile performance as a young woman who has sunk into a drunken stupor and appears to be taken under the wing of a mysterious older figure, Laure (played by the director's muse and wife, Stéphane Audran). Betty confides her painful break from a stultifying bourgeois existence, and her erotic life is presented as something that has left a mark on her. This is one of the more intelligent and perceptive of Simenon film adaptations.

L'Inconnu dans la Maison

France, 1992 (*The Strangers in the House*).
Director: Georges Lautner.
Adaptation: Jean Lartéguy, Georges Lautner and Bernard Stora.
Main actors: Jean-Paul Belmondo, Renée Faure, Cristiana Réali, Sébastien Tavel, François Perrot, Geneviève Page, Pierre Vernier, Jean-Louis Richard, Gaston Vacchia, Muriel Belmondo.

Tsena Golovy

UK/France/Russia/Germany/Ukraine co-production, 1992 (published originally as *Le Prix d'un Homme*, 1980).
Director: Nikolai Ilyinsky.
Adaptation: Nikolai Ilyinsky.

Main actors: Vladimir Samoylov, Lembit Ulfsak, Valentinas Masalskis, Lyubov Polishchuk, Ivars Kalnins.

L'Ours en Peluche

France, 1994 (*Teddy Bear*).
Director: Jacques Deray.
Adaptation: Filippo Ascione, Jean Curtelin and Dardano Sacchetti.
Main actors: Regina Bianchi, Paolo Bonacelli, Martine Brochard, Francesca Dellera, Alain Delon, Julie du Page, Laure Killing.

Comments: Jacques Deray's *L'Ours en Peluche* was released and promoted as a French film, but it sported a bumper crop of Italian talent.

Tangier Cop

UK/USA, 1997, also known as *Heartbreak City* (Simenon is credited, but it is unclear which book it is based on).
Director: Stephen Whittaker.
Adaptation: Julian Bond.
Main actors: Donald Sumpter, Pastora Vega, Sean Chapman, Joe Shaw, David Schofield, John Bowler, Claude Aufaure.

Los de Enfrente

Spain, 1998 (*The People Opposite*).
Director: Jesús Garay.
Adaptation: Jesús Garay.
Main actors: Carme Elías, Ben Gazzara, Juanjo Puigcorbé, Estelle Skornik.

En Plein Cœur

France, 1998 (*In Case of Emergency*).
Director: Pierre Jolivet.
Adaptation: Rose Bosch.
Main actors: Gérard Lanvin, Virginie Ledoyen, Carole Bouquet, Guillaume Canet, Aurélie Vérillon, Jean-Pierre Lorit.

Comments: The film was released in the USA as *In All Innocence*.

Adela

Spain, 2000 (*Tropic Moon*).
Director: Eduardo Mignogna.
Adaptation: Eduardo Mignogna and François-Olivier Rousseau.
Main actors: Eulàlia Ramón, Grégoire Colin, Martin Lamotte, Mario Gas, Isabel Vera, Martín Adjemián.

La Habitación Azul

Mexico/Spain, 2001 (*The Blue Room*).
Director: Walter Doehner.
Adaptation: Walter Doehner and Vicente Leñero.
Main actors: Juan Manuel Bernal, Patricia Llaca, Elena Anaya, Mario Iván Martínez, Margarita Sanz, Damián Alcázar.

Comments: The unhurried pace of this adaptation will not be to every taste and there is a sense that the cast (who will be familiar to viewers who have seen contemporaneous Mexico movies) give efficient rather than inspired performances. The film was sold as being unabashedly sexual, and the erotic advertising in this case was mendacious. There are, however, moments that are worthy of Simenon's original novel.

La Maison du Canal

France/Belgium, 2003 (*The House by the Canal*).
Director: Alain Berliner.
Adaptation: Dominique Garnier and Alain Berliner.
Main actors: Isilde Le Besco, Corentin Lobet, Nicolas Buysse, Jean-Pierre Cassel.

Feux Rouges

France, 2004 (*Red Lights*).
Director: Cédric Kahn,
Adaptation: Cédric Kahn, Laurence Ferreira Barbosa and Gilles Marchand,
Main actors: Jean-Pierre Darroussin, Carole Bouquet, Vincent Deniard.

La Californie

France, 2006 (*Blind Path*).
Director: Jacques Fieschi.
Adaptation: Jacques Fieschi.
Main actors: Nathalie Baye, Mylène Demongeot, Radivoje Bukvic, Ludivine Sagnier, Roschdy Zem.

Monsieur Joseph

France, 2007 (*The Little Man from Archangel*).
Director: Olivier Langlois
Adaptation: Jacques Santamaria.

Main actors: Daniel Prévost, Julie-Marie Parmentier, Serge Riaboukine, Catherine Davenier.

Comments: The best films of Simenon's work are those that fully appreciate the different approaches required for the novelist's very specific takes on particular narratives. The stripped-back original, *The Little Man from Archangel*, is intelligently reproduced in the straightforward story of a specialist bookseller, the eponymous Monsieur Joseph. He was born in Algeria but has successfully integrated himself into French society – until, that is, his young wife goes missing and suspicion falls on him. Writing and acting are perfectly at the service of the narrative here, which examines issues of racism and a community closing against those it perceives as outsiders.

The Man from London (A Londoni Férfi)

Hungary/France/Germany, 2007 (*The Man from London*).
Directors: Béla Tarr and Ágnes Hranitzky.
Adaptation: Béla Tarr and László Krasznahorkai.
Main actors: Miroslav Krobot, Tilda Swinton, János Derzsi, István Lénárt.

Comment: This effort from Hungarian auteur Béla Tarr is surely the slowest and artiest Simenon adaptation ever. Whatever one's ultimate view of the film, with its glacial pace and haunted performances, there is no denying that the grim, oppressive atmosphere of a fog-shrouded port town is conveyed in all its clamminess.

La Chambre Bleue

France, 2014 (*The Blue Room*).
Director: Mathieu Amalric.
Adaptation: Mathieu Amalric and Stéphanie Cléau.
Main actors: Mathieu Amalric, Léa Drucker, Stéphanie Cléau.

Comments: *La Chambre Bleue* is one of the most impressive of recent Simenon adaptations. The film is a triumph for its director-star Mathieu Amalric, who expertly transposes the doom-laden, claustrophobic tone of the source novel.

Les Volets Verts

France, 2022 (*The Heart of a Man*).
Director: Jean Becker.
Adaptation: Jean-Loup Dabadie.
Main actors: Gérard Depardieu, Fanny Ardant, Stéfi Celma, Benoît Poelvoorde.

Maigret on UK Television

The first BBC TV Maigret – now largely forgotten – was the respected actor Basil Sydney in a version of *Maigret and the Dead Girl/Maigret et la Jeune Morte*, under the title *Maigret and the Lost Life*. This adaptation appeared in a popular slot called 'Sunday Night Theatre' in 1959. The novel was adapted by Giles Cooper, with both directing and producing chores handled by Campbell Logan. In the days before long-form TV, Campbell's economical film clocked in at just 75 minutes, with supporting players including Henry Oscar, future Doctor Who Patrick Troughton, Mary Merrall and Andre Van Gyseghem.

It is hardly surprising that this debut appearance of the French detective was eclipsed – and remains so – by a very successful series starring another British actor...

The Rupert Davies Series

Of the many actors who have played Inspector Jules Maigret, Simenon admirers are often intrigued as to who was the author's own favourite. Interestingly, the detective's creator did not choose such French actors as Jean Gabin or Pierre Renoir, who one might have expected to be a shoo-in as first choice. Instead, he selected the British actor Rupert Davies in a much loved TV incarnation that began in 1960. This televisual incarnation of Simenon's immortal detective was so definitive that it remained ensconced as the defining image of the character for generations of viewers in the UK.

While the character actor Rupert Davies created a subtle and well-rounded version of the implacable French copper, the vehicles in which he appeared had less apparent French colour than modern viewers might expect – but the choice of locations was always spot-on (exteriors were frequently shot in Paris). And even though the language spoken was English, viewers quickly accepted the notion that we were watching something indelibly French. In the same way that Jeremy Brett's Sherlock Holmes effectively trounced a legion of highly successful incarnations of the character, the dour but humorous Davies was impeccable casting – and those who reacquaint themselves with his performances or watch them for the first time (the series was unavailable for some considerable time before appearing on DVD in 2021) will quickly realise that Davies was a much more nuanced and interesting actor than one might think, despite sterling work in such supporting roles as the tortured priest he played in Michael Reeves' *Witchfinder General* (1968). While actors as prestigious as Charles Laughton and Jean Gabin used grander, more theatrical flourishes in their versions of Maigret, Davies (and his directors) invariably eschewed a larger-than-life approach – even when, on occasion, the detective loses his temper.

The series was first transmitted in October 1960 and it ran to a respectable 52 episodes before ending in December 1963. However, such was the affection that Davies enjoyed among the British public in his portrayal of Maigret that some six years after the series finished there was also a one-off production, in February 1969, of the Simenon novel *Maigret Defends Himself/ Maigret Se Défend* (retitled for the adaptation as *Maigret at Bay*), with Davies comfortably fitting back into the part. This late flowering of the character was presented as part of the BBC's 'Play of the Month' series.

The earlier episodes were filmed as live studio performances, but the occasional technical insecurities hardly matter, given that the series was clearly doing justice to Simenon's original creation right from the start. Later episodes became more technically adroit, but the considerable success of this British iteration of Simenon was clearly down to the canny casting – not just Rupert Davies in the defining acting job of his career, but a lengthy list of highly capable British supporting players. Series regulars included such accomplished actors as Ewen Solon as the reliable Sergeant Lucas, Helen Shingler in the crucial role of Madame Maigret, Neville Jason very characterful as Lapointe, and Victor Lucas as Torrence.

Andrew Osborn was the executive producer, while a variety of writers and directors handled individual episodes.

Those who have sampled the other iterations of the detective on television and in his various film incarnations are unlikely to argue with the fact that Rupert Davies remains the definitive Maigret. And as a final seal of approval, Georges Simenon once handed the actor one of his novels as a present with the inscription 'At last I have found the perfect Maigret'.

The Michael Gambon Series

The problem of having actors speak English and yet constantly refer to French surnames and street names was well handled in the much acclaimed Michael Gambon series, and many felt that this series did more justice to Simenon's novels than any previous television versions – or, for that matter, the various French film attempts. While Gambon is a master of the large-scale theatrical effect, he is also adept at understatement and observation; these characteristics are fully utilised in the Maigret series, where the more outrageous behaviour is the province of suspects and villains, while Maigret looks coolly on. Gambon, tapping his pipe and observing everything with flickering eyes, is ideal casting.

Like many big men, Gambon is actually rather graceful, and he is particularly good at revealing the psychological state of his character – a real achievement, given that Gambon rarely has the lines (or, for that matter, any obvious physical reactions) to exteriorise what Maigret is feeling. The sense of danger that accompanies the actor is also cleverly utilised; when Gambon appeared on the London stage in Arthur Miller's *A View from the Bridge*, the physical violence with which he seemed to threaten his fellow actors made audiences quake. What also works particularly well in this series is Maigret's understated sympathy for people on the wrong side of the law, and often an antipathy towards his self-important superiors.

Of course, one of the pleasures of watching TV series of this vintage is catching a wealth of acting talent at an early stage in their careers. 'Maigret and the Night Club Dancer', for instance, features an ill-fated stripper played by a pre-Hollywood Minnie Driver, while her blowsy, chain-smoking boss is played by Brenda Blethyn. The same episode also has the now much acclaimed British actor Michael Sheen as a jittery drug addict. More regular roles were played by Jack Galloway (Janvier), James Larkin (Lapointe) and John Moffatt (Coméliau). Ciaran Madden played Madame Maigret in the first six episodes, and Barbara Flynn played her in the second six. But however adroit the supporting cast, it's Michael Gambon we never take our eyes off.

While the production values are modest, there is always a convincing Gallic feel to the proceedings, even though Budapest stood in for Paris. Some of the episodes deal with the limitations by adopting the classic restricted settings beloved of crime writers; these include 'The Patience of Maigret', which takes place in an apartment building, and 'Maigret and the Hotel Majestic', one of the more atmospheric episodes. The series ran on UK television for two seasons in 1992 and 1993. It was produced for Granada TV by Paul Marcus, and the various directors and writers hired for the series made no missteps in the translation of Simenon's narratives to the screen.

The Rowan Atkinson Series

The phrase is familiar: the clown who wants to play Hamlet. And while Rowan Atkinson is generally regarded as one of Britain's most successful comic actors, eyebrows were raised when he announced that he wanted to tackle Georges Simenon's legendary French copper. Atkinson had demonstrated a certain range with his characterisations (although directors tended to indulge him and encourage grotesquely over-the-top performances – as in the James Bond film *Never Say Never Again*), but many were open-minded and prepared to give his Maigret the benefit of the doubt. Until, that is, they saw his first assumption of the role. The problem with this misfiring series of adaptations was very easy to spot. Atkinson was trying very strenuously to submerge his comic persona, and accordingly presented a singularly dour Inspector Maigret, with what little humour was allowed the character falling absolutely flat. The result, of course, was a siphoning off of the understated sardonic edge that the best performers had brought to the part, from Jean Gabin to Rupert Davies and Michael Gambon. Audience response was distinctly underwhelming, and it is hardly surprising that the series was finally cancelled, despite some capable playing for the other characters.

BBC Radio Four Maigret Series

And finally, Maigret on radio rather than television. This series, first broadcast in August 1976 and with the last episode airing in August 1977, was set within the framework of Maigret recalling his cases in retirement in an imagined conversation with the author Georges Simenon. Maurice Denham played

Maigret and Michael Gough played Simenon throughout the series. Despite the presence of two consummate actors, the series rarely comes to life; in fact, like many radio dramas, it sounds rather as if the script is being read by rote. There is also much condensation and the elimination of many characters and scenes, although the overall narratives remain faithful to the main plots of the novels.

Acknowledgements

I would like to thank the following for their help (in various ways – from conversations to general inspiration to comments and other things). In particular, Howard Curtis (my friend of many decades, and one of the most insightful translators of Simenon at work today), Maxim Jakubowski, Josephine Greywoode, Alison Joseph, Mike Ashley, Ros Schwartz, Fiona Livesey, Christopher Sinclair-Stevenson, R. N. Morris, John Simenon, Siân Reynolds, Kim Newman, Boyd Tonkin, Andrew Martin, Andy Lawrence, my publisher Ion Mills, and, of course, the late David Carter for his Trojan efforts.

Index of Titles

247

INDEX OF TITLES